# APPLIED MACHINE LEARNING

# APPLIED MACHINE LEARNING

**Sasirekha R., Jemshia Miriam, Surya V.**

KHANNA BOOK PUBLISHING CO. (P) Ltd.
4C/4344, Ansari Road, Darya Ganj, New Delhi, India

Sathyabama Institute of Science and Technology
Jeppiaar Nagar, Rajiv Gandhi Salai, Chennai, Tamilnadu, India

Dear Readers,

To prevent the piracy, this book is secured with HIGH SECURITY HOLOGRAM on the front title cover. In case you don't find the hologram on the front cover title, please write us to at contact@khannabooks.com or whatsapp us at +91-99109 09320 and avail special gift voucher for yourself.

Specimen of Hologram on front Cover title:

Moreover, there is a SPECIAL DISCOUNT COUPON for you with EVERY HOLOGRAM.

How to avail this SPECIAL DISCOUNT:

Step 1: Scratch the hologram
Step 2: Under the scratch area, your "coupon code" is available
Step 3: Logon to www.khannabooks.com
Step 4: Use your "coupon code" in the shopping cart and get your copy at a special discount
Step 5: Enjoy your reading!

Thanks,
Khanna Publishing House

**ISBN:** 978-93-55388-42-1

**Applied Machine Learning**
*by* **Sasirekha R., Surya V., Jemshia Miriam**

**First Edition:** 2025

To view complete list of books, please scan the QR Code:

*Published by:*
**Khanna Book Publishing Co. (P) Ltd.**
CIN: U22110DL1998PTC095547

Visit us at: www.khannabooks.com
Write us at: contact@khannabooks.com

Printed in Bharat.

# Preface

Machine learning has become an essential tool in solving complex problems across various domains, from healthcare and finance to autonomous systems and natural language processing. As data continues to grow exponentially, the ability to build models that learn from data and make intelligent predictions is more critical than ever. This book begins with the foundational principles of machine learning, covering key concepts such as supervised and unsupervised learning, feature engineering, and model evaluation. Readers will gain a deep understanding of essential algorithms, including linear regression, decision trees, support vector machines, and neural networks. Each concept is explained with clear examples and mathematical intuition, ensuring that both beginners and experienced practitioners can follow along and build a strong conceptual framework.

A key focus of this book is on practical implementation. Using Python and popular machine learning libraries such as Scikit-learn, TensorFlow, and PyTorch, we provide step-by-step coding examples and real-world case studies. Readers will learn how to preprocess data, tune hyperparameters, optimize models, and deploy machine learning solutions effectively. By working through hands-on projects, they will develop the skills necessary to apply machine learning to real-world datasets and business problems.

Beyond model development, this book also explores critical challenges in applied machine learning, such as bias in data, model interpretability, scalability, and ethical considerations. With the increasing impact of AI-driven decisions on society, it is crucial to understand how to build responsible and transparent models. We emphasize best practices for ensuring fairness, accountability, and reliability in machine learning applications.

This book is intended for students, professionals, and researchers who want to deepen their knowledge of machine learning and its applications. Whether you are an aspiring data scientist, a software engineer looking to integrate ML into applications, or a business leader aiming to leverage AI-driven insights, this book will serve as a comprehensive guide. We invite you to embark on this exciting journey into applied machine learning and discover its potential to transform industries and drive innovation.

# Contents

❖❖❖

Unit 1

# Introduction to Applied Machine Learning

## Rationale

Data acquisition is an important step in any data acquiring process, ensuring the collection of accurate, relevant, and high-quality data for analysis. It frames the foundation for machine learning, research, and decision-making by collecting raw data from various sources such as sensors, databases, or user inputs. Effective data acquisition improves model performance, enhances predictive accuracy, and minimizes biases. In fields like sentiment analysis, properly acquired data enables meaningful insights and reliable outcomes. Without structured and efficient data acquisition, subsequent stages—such as preprocessing, modeling, and interpretation—are compromised, leading to inaccurate or misleading results.

## 1.1 INTRODUCTION

Applied machine learning refers to the practical use of machine learning (ML) algorithms to solve real-world problems across various industries. It bridges the gap between theoretical research in machine learning and its implementation in real applications. The goal is to design systems that can learn from data, make predictions, recognize patterns, and even make autonomous decisions based on data analysis. With advancements in computing power, access to large datasets, and improvements in algorithmic design, machine learning has become a pivotal tool in solving complex problems.

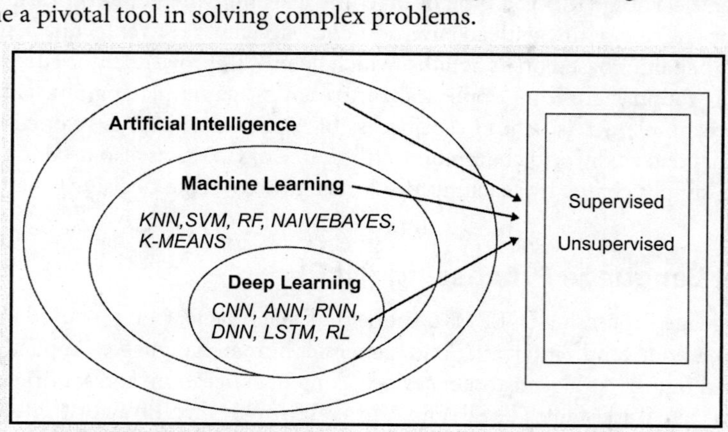


***Fig.1.1*** *Learning Classification*

---

*Figure.1.1 depicts the classification of learning methodologies.*

## 2. Real-World Applications

Machine learning is applied in a wide array of sectors, from healthcare to finance, retail to transportation. For instance, in healthcare, ML is used for predicting disease outbreaks, diagnosing medical conditions, and personalizing treatment plans. In finance, it plays a critical role in fraud detection, risk assessment, and algorithmic trading. In transportation, autonomous vehicles are powered by ML models that help them navigate, avoid collisions, and optimize routes. As these technologies advance, they continue to transform industries, making them more efficient and cost-effective.

## 3. Supervised Learning in Applied ML

Supervised learning is one of the most common paradigms in applied machine learning. It involves training a model on labeled data, where the input features and their corresponding output labels are provided. The model learns to map inputs to the correct outputs based on patterns in the data. Applications of supervised learning are vast, ranging from image classification (e.g., identifying objects in pictures) to speech recognition (translating voice commands into text). Algorithms like decision trees, support vector machines, and deep neural networks are often used in these applications.

## 4. Unsupervised Learning in Applied ML

Unsupervised learning, on the other hand, deals with unlabeled data. The model tries to uncover hidden patterns and structures in the data without explicit output labels. Clustering and dimensionality reduction are common unsupervised learning tasks. For example, in customer segmentation, businesses use unsupervised learning algorithms to group customers based on purchasing behavior, demographics, and preferences. Principal component analysis (PCA) and k-means clustering are frequently used techniques. Unsupervised learning helps extract insights and understand complex datasets that don't have clear labels or outcomes.

## 5. Reinforcement Learning in Applied ML

Reinforcement learning (RL) is a type of machine learning where an agent learns how to make decisions by interacting with an environment. The agent receives feedback in the form of rewards or penalties based on its actions, which helps it improve its future decisions. This technique has found significant application in robotics, game playing, and autonomous systems. For example, RL is behind the success of AlphaGo, the AI developed by Google DeepMind that defeated world champions in the game of Go. RL is also used in optimizing logistics and supply chains by teaching machines how to make decisions that maximize efficiency.

## 6. Natural Language Processing (NLP)

Natural Language Processing (NLP) is a subfield of machine learning focused on enabling machines to understand, interpret, and generate human language. Applied NLP has revolutionized industries like customer service, content generation, and sentiment analysis. Chatbots and virtual assistants like Siri and Alexa rely heavily on NLP algorithms to interpret spoken language and provide meaningful responses. Additionally, sentiment analysis tools use NLP to monitor social media and gauge public sentiment around products, services, or events. NLP's application in machine translation (e.g., Google Translate) is another area where its impact is highly visible.

### 7. Machine Learning in Predictive Analytics

Predictive analytics is one of the most prominent applications of machine learning. In this context, ML algorithms analyze historical data to make predictions about future events or trends. This approach is commonly applied in marketing for customer churn prediction, in finance for forecasting stock prices, and in supply chain management for inventory optimization. Regression models, time series analysis, and ensemble methods are frequently used to build predictive models that provide actionable insights. Predictive analytics empowers businesses and organizations to make data-driven decisions, reduce risks, and improve outcomes.

### 8. Challenges in Applied Machine Learning

Despite its potential, the application of machine learning faces several challenges. One major issue is the quality and quantity of data available for training models. Insufficient or biased data can lead to inaccurate predictions and perpetuate systemic biases in automated systems. Additionally, model interpretability is a concern, particularly in fields like healthcare, where understanding why a model made a specific decision is crucial. Other challenges include the computational cost of training complex models and the risk of overfitting, where models perform well on training data but fail to generalize to new, unseen data.

### 9. Ethics and Fairness in Machine Learning

Ethical concerns are increasingly important in the applied machine learning space. The use of ML algorithms in areas such as criminal justice, hiring, and loan approval raises questions about fairness, bias, and accountability. For example, facial recognition systems have been criticized for being less accurate in identifying people of certain racial backgrounds, leading to concerns about discrimination. Ensuring that machine learning models are transparent, unbiased, and aligned with ethical principles is a growing area of research and regulatory concern. Organizations must take steps to mitigate bias and ensure that their ML systems are fair and responsible.

### 10. Future of Applied Machine Learning

The future of applied machine learning is both exciting and full of potential. With the development of more advanced algorithms, increased computing power, and the availability of big data, machine learning will continue to advance in scope and capability. Future applications may include more sophisticated forms of artificial intelligence in areas such as autonomous systems, personalized medicine, and climate change modeling. The continued integration of machine learning into everyday life will lead to smarter technologies, more personalized experiences, and potentially revolutionary changes in how industries operate. However, as these technologies evolve, ensuring they are deployed responsibly and ethically will be critical.

## 1.2 TOWARDS INTELLIGENT MACHINES

An ultimate challenge for science is to create intelligent machines that emulate human intelligence.

Information repositories are collecting a myriad of information capturing operational experience in diverse fields.

The collected information may be categorized on the basis of nature of experience:

- Experimental data (examples, samples, measurements, records, patterns or observations).
- Structured human knowledge (experience, expertise, heuristics) expressed in linguistic form (IF-THEN rules).

Whenever devising "mathematical/statistical model is feasible using a reasonable number of equations" that can solve the given problem in a reasonable time, at a reasonable cost, and with reasonable accuracy, there is no need to look for an alternative.

**The basic premises of machine learning are as follows:**

The real world is pervasively imprecise and uncertain. The precision and certainty carry a cost.

A computer program is said to learn from experience with respect to some class of tasks and performance measure, if the performance at the tasks, as measured by performance measure, improves with the experience.

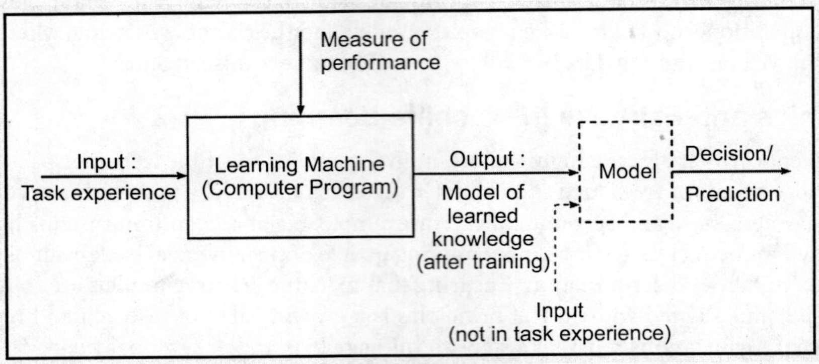


***Fig 1.2.** Representation of machine learning*

*Figure.1.2 shows the representation of machine learning*

## 1.3 DATA REPRESENTATIONS

### 1. Introduction to Data Representation in Applied Machine Learning

Data representation refers to the way information is structured and presented for machine learning models to understand and process. In applied machine learning, data is typically represented in formats that capture the essential features and patterns that models need to learn. Effective data representation is key to the success of machine learning tasks, as it determines how well a model can generalize and make predictions. The quality of the data representation often has a direct impact on the performance of machine learning algorithms.

### 2. Structured vs. Unstructured Data

Data in machine learning can generally be categorized into two types: structured and unstructured. Structured data refers to information that is organized in a fixed format, typically in rows and columns, such as spreadsheets or databases. This type of data is easier to represent and analyze using traditional algorithms. Examples include numerical data (e.g., sales figures) and categorical data (e.g., customer demographics). On the other hand, unstructured data refers to information that lacks a predefined format, such as text, images, and audio. Unstructured data requires more complex methods for representation, such as vectorization for text or pixel grids for images.

## 3. Feature Engineering and Data Transformation

Feature engineering is the process of selecting, modifying, or creating new features from raw data to improve the performance of machine learning models. This process involves transforming the data into a more suitable format by removing noise, normalizing values, or extracting meaningful patterns. For example, in time series data, features like trends, seasonality, or moving averages might be extracted. In text data, techniques such as stemming, stopword removal, or TF-IDF (Term Frequency-Inverse Document Frequency) can be used to convert raw text into structured features. Effective feature engineering can greatly enhance the learning capacity of machine learning models.

## 4. One-Hot Encoding for Categorical Data

In applied machine learning, categorical data often needs to be converted into a format that algorithms can process. One of the most common techniques for this is one-hot encoding. This method transforms categorical variables into a binary vector, where each category is represented as a separate column with a 1 or 0 indicating whether the category is present. For example, the categorical variable "Color" with values {Red, Blue, Green} could be represented as three binary columns: [1, 0, 0] for Red, [0, 1, 0] for Blue, and [0, 0, 1] for Green. One-hot encoding is particularly useful for machine learning algorithms that cannot process categorical data directly.

## 5. Embedding Representations for High-Dimensional Data

In situations where data has high dimensionality, such as when working with text or images, traditional methods like one-hot encoding may not be sufficient. Instead, embedding representations are used to map high-dimensional data to a lower-dimensional space. Word embeddings like Word2Vec, GloVe, or fastText, for example, represent words as dense vectors where semantically similar words have similar representations. These embeddings enable models to capture contextual relationships between words, making them more effective in tasks like sentiment analysis, translation, and question-answering. Image data can also be represented through deep learning models like convolutional neural networks (CNNs), which learn hierarchical features that capture essential information about images.

## 6. Normalization and Scaling of Numerical Data

Normalization and scaling are essential steps in data representation, particularly when dealing with numerical data. Machine learning algorithms like gradient descent are sensitive to the scale of the data, and features with large ranges can dominate the learning process, leading to poor performance. Normalization (rescaling data to a range, e.g., 0 to 1) and standardization (transforming data to have a mean of 0 and a standard deviation of 1) are common techniques used to ensure that all features contribute equally to the model's performance. These methods are particularly important for algorithms like k-nearest neighbors (KNN) or support vector machines (SVM), which are sensitive to the distance between data points.

### 7. Handling Missing Data in Representation

Missing data is a common issue in applied machine learning, and how it is handled during data representation can significantly affect model performance. There are several strategies for dealing with missing data, such as imputation (filling in missing values with mean, median, or mode values), deletion (removing rows or columns with missing values), or using algorithms that can handle missing data directly. In some cases, missing values might themselves contain valuable information. For example, the absence of certain features might indicate a specific class or behavior. Therefore, understanding the context of missing data and choosing an appropriate method for representation is crucial.

### 8. Time Series Data Representation

Time series data, which consists of observations collected at regular time intervals, requires special attention in terms of data representation. This type of data is characterized by temporal dependencies, meaning that past observations influence future ones. In applied machine learning, time series data is often represented using techniques like lag features, rolling statistics (e.g., moving averages), and time-based transformations (e.g., extracting the day of the week or the month). For more complex tasks, recurrent neural networks (RNNs) or long short-term memory networks (LSTMs) are often employed, as they are designed to handle sequential data and capture long-term dependencies.

### 9. Graph Data Representation

In certain machine learning applications, such as social networks, recommendation systems, or molecular chemistry, data is represented as graphs. A graph consists of nodes (representing entities) and edges (representing relationships between entities). Graph-based machine learning techniques, such as Graph Neural Networks (GNNs), allow for the representation and analysis of data where relationships between entities are key. For example, in social networks, users are represented as nodes, and the connections between them (e.g., friendships) are represented as edges. Graph-based methods can uncover complex patterns and relationships that would be difficult to capture with traditional data representations.

### 10. The Role of Data Representation in Model Performance

The way data is represented plays a crucial role in the performance of machine learning models. A well-chosen data representation can help models capture the underlying structure and patterns in the data, leading to more accurate predictions. In contrast, poor data representation can hinder model performance, even if advanced algorithms are used. It is important to experiment with different representations, understand the nature of the data, and tailor the representation to the specific problem at hand. Ultimately, effective data representation is an iterative process that involves understanding both the raw data and the algorithmic requirements, ensuring the two are aligned for optimal performance.

## 1.4 FORMS OF LEARNING IN APPLIED MACHINE LEARNING

In applied machine learning, the process of learning involves how algorithms acquire knowledge from data to make predictions or decisions. Different forms of learning are used depending on the problem, the nature of the data, and the goals of the system. The primary forms of learning in machine learning include supervised learning, unsupervised learning, semi-supervised learning, reinforcement learning, and deep learning. Each of these forms has unique characteristics, applications, and challenges, and understanding them is key to choosing the appropriate method for specific tasks.

## 1. Supervised Learning

Supervised learning is one of the most widely used forms of learning, where a model is trained on labeled data, meaning the input data comes with corresponding target values or labels. The goal of supervised learning is to learn a mapping function from the input data to the correct output labels. Common examples of supervised learning include classification tasks, such as identifying whether an email is spam or not, and regression tasks, such as predicting house prices. Algorithms like decision trees, support vector machines (SVM), and neural networks are frequently used in supervised learning.

## 2. Unsupervised Learning

Unsupervised learning is a form of machine learning where the model is trained on data without labeled outcomes or target variables. The goal of unsupervised learning is to find hidden structures, patterns, or relationships within the data. Common tasks in unsupervised learning include clustering, where the model groups data points based on similarity (e.g., customer segmentation in marketing), and dimensionality reduction, where high-dimensional data is reduced to fewer features for easier analysis (e.g., principal component analysis). Algorithms like k-means clustering, hierarchical clustering, and principal component analysis (PCA) are often used.

## 3. Semi-Supervised Learning

Semi-supervised learning is a hybrid approach that falls between supervised and unsupervised learning. In this form, the model is trained on a small amount of labeled data alongside a large amount of unlabeled data. Semi-supervised learning is especially useful when acquiring labeled data is expensive or time-consuming, but a large amount of unlabeled data is available. For example, in medical image analysis, labeling each image can be costly, but many images without labels can be collected. Semi-supervised learning methods, such as self-training, co-training, and graph-based methods, can leverage both labeled and unlabeled data to improve model performance.

## 4. Reinforcement Learning

Reinforcement learning (RL) is a type of machine learning where an agent learns by interacting with an environment and receiving feedback in the form of rewards or penalties based on its actions. The goal is to find a sequence of actions that maximize cumulative rewards over time. RL is commonly used in applications such as robotics, game playing, autonomous driving, and recommendation systems. Algorithms like Q-learning, deep Q-networks (DQN), and policy gradient methods are commonly applied in reinforcement learning tasks, where the system continuously learns from its experiences.

## 5. Self-Supervised Learning

Self-supervised learning is a subfield of machine learning where the model generates its own supervision or labels from the data. The model typically uses part of the data to predict other parts of the same data. For example, in natural language processing, models like BERT use self-supervised learning by predicting missing words in sentences as part of training. This approach can be seen as a form of unsupervised learning because the model is not given explicit labels but creates its own learning signal, allowing it to learn useful representations from large datasets with minimal labeled data.

### 6. Transfer Learning

Transfer learning is a technique where a model developed for a specific task is reused for a different but related task. Instead of training a model from scratch, transfer learning leverages the knowledge gained from a previously trained model on a large dataset and applies it to a smaller dataset. This method is particularly useful in domains like image recognition and natural language processing, where pre-trained models (e.g., ResNet, BERT) can be fine-tuned to specific tasks with minimal data. Transfer learning speeds up training and improves performance when labeled data is scarce.

### 7. Active Learning

Active learning is a form of machine learning where the model actively selects the most informative data points from a pool of unlabeled data and requests labels for those data points. This is useful in situations where labeling data is expensive or time-consuming, as the model can prioritize the data points that will help it improve the most. Active learning is often used in combination with supervised learning, where the model iteratively queries the oracle (e.g., a human expert) for labels, thus reducing the need for large amounts of labeled data.

### 8. Online Learning

Online learning is a form of learning where the model is trained incrementally on data that arrives in a stream. Unlike traditional batch learning, where the model is trained on the entire dataset at once, online learning updates the model continuously as new data becomes available. This is particularly useful in real-time applications such as stock market prediction, fraud detection, and recommendation systems, where data is constantly evolving. Algorithms such as stochastic gradient descent (SGD) and online variants of machine learning models are commonly used in online learning scenarios.

### 9. Ensemble Learning

Ensemble learning is a technique where multiple models (often of different types) are combined to improve performance. The idea is that by aggregating the predictions of several models, the system can achieve better accuracy and generalization than any individual model. Common ensemble methods include bagging (e.g., Random Forest), boosting (e.g., AdaBoost, Gradient Boosting Machines), and stacking, where a meta-model is trained to combine the outputs of base models. Ensemble learning is widely used in applied machine learning for tasks like classification and regression.

### 10. Deep Learning

Deep learning is a subset of machine learning that focuses on algorithms inspired by the structure and function of the human brain. It uses multi-layered neural networks to learn complex representations from large amounts of data. Deep learning has shown remarkable success in areas such as image and speech recognition, natural language processing, and game playing. Convolutional neural networks (CNNs) are typically used for image processing, while recurrent neural networks (RNNs) and transformers are used in sequence-based tasks like language modeling. Deep learning models are known for their ability to automatically extract features from raw data, making them highly effective for tasks with unstructured data.

### 11. Few-Shot Learning

Few-shot learning is a form of machine learning where a model is trained to perform tasks with only a small number of labeled examples. This is especially important when dealing with situations where acquiring large datasets is difficult or expensive. Few-shot learning aims to develop models that can generalize from a few examples, often relying on techniques like transfer learning, meta-learning, or data augmentation. This approach has applications in areas like medical diagnosis, where rare diseases may only have a few recorded instances, but the model must still be able to make accurate predictions.

### 12. Multi-Task Learning

Multi-task learning is an approach where a model is trained on several related tasks simultaneously. The idea is that by learning multiple tasks at the same time, the model can leverage shared knowledge and improve performance on each task. For example, in computer vision, a model could learn to classify objects and simultaneously predict the location of those objects (object detection). Multi-task learning is useful when tasks share common features, and training on multiple tasks helps the model generalize better across different domains.

### 13. Federated Learning

Federated learning is a form of machine learning where data remains decentralized, and the model is trained across multiple devices (e.g., smartphones) or servers while keeping the data on the local devices. The model learns by aggregating updates from each device without the need to transfer raw data to a central server. This approach is especially useful for privacy-sensitive applications, such as medical research or personal assistants, where sharing sensitive data may be a concern. Federated learning helps improve model performance while ensuring data privacy and security.

### 14. Evolving Forms of Learning

Machine learning is a dynamic field, with new forms of learning continuously emerging. As the field advances, new learning paradigms, such as meta-learning and neuromorphic computing, promise to further revolutionize how machines learn and adapt to new environments. The choice of learning approach in applied machine learning depends on the specific task, the nature of the data, and the resources available. Understanding the different forms of learning is essential for selecting the most appropriate method to solve complex, real-world problems effectively.

## 1.5 BASIC LINEAR ALGEBRA IN MACHINE LEARNING

Linear algebra is the foundation of many machine learning algorithms. It provides mathematical tools for representing and manipulating data, making it essential for tasks like data preprocessing, model optimization, and dimensionality reduction. Below, we explore key concepts of linear algebra in machine learning, along with examples.

## 1. Scalars, Vectors, Matrices, and Tensors

Linear algebra involves working with different types of mathematical objects:

- **Scalars**: Single numerical values (e.g., 5, -3, 0.7).
- **Vectors**: Ordered lists of numbers representing points in space.
- **Matrices**: 2D arrays of numbers.
- **Tensors**: Generalized matrices extending to more than two dimensions.
- **Example:** A grayscale image can be represented as a matrix, while a colored image is a 3D tensor.

## 2. Vector Operations in Machine Learning

Vectors play a crucial role in ML, representing **features** of data points. Common vector operations include:

- **Addition**
- **Dot Product:** Measures similarity between two vectors
    - **Use Case:** Dot products are used in **cosine similarity** for text analysis.

## 3. Matrices and Machine Learning Models

A matrix can store large datasets where each row represents a data point, and each column is a feature. In ML, matrices are used to represent datasets, weight parameters in neural networks, and transformation functions.

## 4. Matrix Multiplication in Neural Networks

Matrix multiplication is fundamental in deep learning, particularly in **forward and backward propagation**. The multiplication of a matrix (input features) by another matrix (weights) produces predictions.

## 5. Determinant and Inverse of a Matrix

The **determinant** of a square matrix helps determine whether the matrix is invertible. The **inverse** of a matrix is used in solving linear equations.

## 6. Eigenvalues and Eigenvectors in Dimensionality Reduction

Eigenvalues and eigenvectors are used in **Principal Component Analysis (PCA)** to reduce data dimensionality while retaining important patterns. **Example:** In **PCA**, the covariance matrix's eigenvectors define new axes (principal components) that maximize variance.

## 7. Singular Value Decomposition (SVD) in Machine Learning

SVD decomposes a matrix into three matrices, revealing its essential properties. It is widely used in **recommendation systems, noise reduction, and latent semantic analysis (LSA) in NLP. Example:** Netflix uses SVD to analyze **user-movie rating matrices** and recommend films.

## 8. Gradient Descent and Linear Algebra

Gradient descent is an optimization algorithm that uses linear algebra to adjust model parameters iteratively, minimizing errors. It relies on matrix operations and derivatives.

### 9. Norms and Distance Metrics in ML

Vector norms measure magnitude, while distance metrics help classify or cluster data points.

- L1 Norm (Manhattan Distance)
- L2 Norm (Euclidean Distance)
    - **Use Case: L2 norm** is used in regularization techniques like **Ridge Regression.**

Linear algebra is the mathematical backbone of machine learning. From **vector operations, matrix manipulations, eigenvalues, and SVD to optimization techniques like gradient descent**, these concepts power everything from simple regression models to deep neural networks. Understanding linear algebra is essential for implementing efficient and scalable ML algorithms.

## 1.6 LEARNING FROM OBSERVATIONS, BIAS AND VARIANCE, AND OCCAM'S RAZOR PRINCIPLE

Machine learning models aim to learn patterns from observed data to make predictions or decisions. However, the quality of learning depends on how well a model generalizes beyond the given data. This discussion covers three key aspects: **learning from observations, the bias-variance tradeoff, and Occam's Razor principle**, all of which contribute to developing effective models.

### 1. Learning from Observations in Machine Learning

Machine learning is fundamentally about extracting knowledge from data. **Observations** are examples or instances used to train a model, typically consisting of **input features (X)** and corresponding **output labels (Y)**. The learning process involves mapping inputs to outputs by finding underlying relationships within the data. **Example:** In spam email detection, the model learns from past observations of emails labeled as **spam** or **not spam** based on word frequency, sender information, and other characteristics.

### 2. The Importance of Data in Learning

The accuracy and efficiency of learning depend on the **quality, quantity, and diversity** of observations. If a dataset is incomplete or biased, the model may fail to generalize to new data. This highlights the importance of using **representative datasets** and **handling missing values** appropriately. **Example:** A facial recognition model trained only on **light-skinned faces** may struggle to identify people with **darker skin tones**, demonstrating **biased learning from observations**.

### 3. Bias in Machine Learning Models

Bias refers to **systematic errors** in a model due to incorrect assumptions. A model with **high bias** oversimplifies patterns, leading to underfitting. **Underfitting** occurs when the model fails to capture important trends in data, resulting in poor accuracy. **Example:** A linear regression model attempting to fit a complex non-linear dataset will **underfit**, as it assumes a simple straight-line relationship between input and output.

### 4. Variance in Machine Learning Models

Variance measures how much a model's predictions fluctuate based on different training datasets. A **high variance model** overfits the data by capturing noise instead of general patterns. **Overfitting** leads to excellent performance on training data but poor performance on unseen data. **Example:** A deep neural network trained on a small dataset may memorize all training points but fail to make accurate predictions on new data.

## 5. The Bias-Variance Tradeoff

The **bias-variance tradeoff** is a fundamental challenge in machine learning. A model should **balance bias and variance** to achieve optimal generalization.

- **High bias, low variance:** Simple models (e.g., linear regression) that underfit data.
- **Low bias, high variance:** Complex models (e.g., deep neural networks) that overfit data.
- **Optimal model:** A balance where the model captures meaningful patterns while avoiding overfitting.

**Example:** Decision trees with too many splits have **high variance**, while shallow decision trees may **underfit** due to **high bias.**

## 6. Regularization to Control Bias and Variance

Regularization techniques like **Lasso (L1) and Ridge (L2) regression** help control model complexity and prevent overfitting. These methods add a **penalty term** to the loss function, discouraging extreme parameter values and improving generalization.

**Example:** Ridge regression adds a **penalty on large coefficients**, reducing the likelihood of overfitting.

## 7. Occam's Razor Principle in Machine Learning

Occam's Razor states that **simpler models are preferable to complex ones if both explain the data equally well**. This principle suggests that unnecessary complexity increases the risk of overfitting and reduces interpretability.

**Example:** A neural network with **hundreds of layers** might fit training data perfectly, but a **simpler model** with fewer layers may perform just as well while being computationally efficient.

## 8. The Role of Model Complexity

Occam's Razor warns against over-complicating models without justification. While **complex models can capture intricate patterns**, they also introduce noise and increase computation costs. The key is to find the simplest model that still achieves good performance.

**Example:** In text classification, a **Naïve Bayes classifier** may perform well without requiring deep learning, following Occam's Razor.

## 9. Finding the Right Balance

Machine learning practitioners must **balance simplicity, accuracy, and computational efficiency**. Techniques like **cross-validation** and **hyperparameter tuning** help select models that adhere to Occam's Razor while avoiding underfitting.

**Example:** A **random forest** model with 100 trees might not improve much over one with 10 trees but would require significantly more computational power.

Learning from observations is the foundation of machine learning, but models must balance **bias and variance** to generalize well. Occam's Razor encourages using **simpler**

**models** when possible to improve interpretability and efficiency. By understanding these principles, machine learning practitioners can develop models that perform reliably in real-world applications.

## 1.7 INDUCTIVE LEARNING, ESTIMATING GENERALIZATION ERRORS, AND METRICS

Machine learning relies on **inductive learning**, where models learn from specific examples and generalize patterns to unseen data. The effectiveness of a model depends on how well it explores possible hypotheses, estimates generalization errors, and uses appropriate metrics to evaluate performance.

Below, we explore each concept in detail.

### 1. Search in Inductive Learning

Inductive learning is the process of finding patterns from observed data and applying them to new instances. In this approach, a model searches through a **hypothesis space** to find the best function that maps inputs to outputs. This search can be **guided or unguided**, depending on whether we provide prior knowledge or let the model explore freely.

**Example:** In **decision tree learning**, the algorithm searches for the optimal way to split the dataset by minimizing **entropy** or maximizing **information gain**. The tree grows by exploring different splits and selecting the one that best improves classification.

There are different strategies for searching in inductive learning, such as:

- **Exhaustive Search:** Evaluating all possible hypotheses (impractical for large datasets).
- **Heuristic Search:** Using strategies like **gradient descent** or **genetic algorithms** to efficiently explore hypothesis space.

The challenge in inductive learning is to balance **exploration (searching for better models)** and **exploitation (choosing the best-known model so far)** to avoid underfitting or overfitting.

### 2. Challenges in Searching for the Best Model

A major difficulty in inductive learning is dealing with the **bias-variance tradeoff** while searching for an optimal model. If the search process is too restrictive, it may lead to a **high-bias model (underfitting)** that fails to capture patterns in data. On the other hand, an excessively flexible search can lead to **high variance (overfitting)**, where the model memorizes the training data instead of generalizing from it.

**Example:** In **neural networks**, increasing the number of hidden layers expands the search space, potentially improving accuracy. However, without proper **regularization** (e.g., dropout, L2 regularization), the model may overfit.

To make the search process efficient, techniques such as **early stopping, cross-validation, and pruning** are used to prevent overfitting and ensure the model generalizes well to unseen data.

### 3. Estimating Generalization Errors

Generalization error measures how well a model performs on new, unseen data. It is estimated using techniques like **train-test splitting, cross-validation, and bootstrapping**.

The goal is to ensure that the model's performance is not just good on the training set but also on unseen real-world data. There are two types of errors to consider:

- **Training Error:** The error a model makes on the dataset it was trained on.
- **Generalization Error:** The error the model makes on new, unseen data.

**Example:** A machine learning model trained on historical **stock market data** may perform well on past data but fail on future data due to **changing market trends**. This is why **estimating generalization errors** is crucial in financial predictions.

A common way to estimate generalization error is **k-fold cross-validation**, where the dataset is split into **k subsets**, and the model is trained and tested multiple times to get an average error estimate.

## 4. Metrics for Evaluating Machine Learning Models

To measure the effectiveness of a model, we use **evaluation metrics** that provide insights into its accuracy, precision, and ability to generalize. The choice of metric depends on the problem type:

- **Classification Metrics**: Used when the target variable is categorical. Common metrics include:
  - ❖ **Accuracy** = (Correct Predictions) / (Total Predictions)
  - ❖ **Precision & Recall** (important for imbalanced datasets)
  - ❖ **F1-score** (harmonic mean of precision and recall)
- **Regression Metrics**: Used for predicting continuous values. Common metrics include:
  - ❖ **Mean Squared Error (MSE)**: Measures average squared errors.
  - ❖ **Root Mean Squared Error (RMSE)**: Provides an interpretable error in the original scale.
  - ❖ **R-squared ($R^2$)**: Measures how well the model explains the variance in the data.

**Example:** In medical diagnosis, **accuracy** alone is insufficient because false negatives can be deadly. **Precision, recall, and F1-score** help ensure the model prioritizes detecting true positive cases (e.g., cancer detection).

## 5. Importance of Proper Model Evaluation

Choosing the right evaluation metric and accurately estimating generalization error helps in selecting the best model for a given task. Relying on a single metric can be misleading, so practitioners often use multiple evaluation criteria. **Example:** In fraud detection, a model may achieve **99% accuracy** by predicting "not fraud" for most cases, but this would be useless. Instead, **recall and F1-score** are better measures since they focus on correctly identifying fraudulent transactions.

Proper evaluation also helps in **hyperparameter tuning**, where adjustments to learning rate, model depth, and other parameters are tested to optimize performance. By continuously **monitoring error estimates and metrics**, machine learning models can be improved for real-world deployment.

Inductive learning involves searching for the best hypothesis that generalizes well from observations. Estimating **generalization error** ensures the model's performance is not misleadingly good on training data alone. Finally, selecting the right **evaluation metrics** is critical to ensuring that the model is effective for its intended application. Together, these elements form the foundation for building reliable machine learning systems.

## UNIT SUMMARY

- This unit provides a foundational understanding of **applied machine learning**, covering essential concepts that guide the development of intelligent models. The introduction highlights the significance of machine learning in various real-world applications, emphasizing its ability to automate decision-making and enhance predictive accuracy. As we move towards **intelligent machines**, the unit explores how AI-driven systems process and learn from data, enabling advancements in diverse fields such as healthcare, finance, and autonomous systems.
- A critical aspect of machine learning is **data representation**, where different formats, including structured and unstructured data, impact model performance. The unit then discusses **various learning paradigms**, including supervised, unsupervised, semi-supervised, and reinforcement learning, each playing a vital role in different problem-solving scenarios. Additionally, **basic linear algebra concepts**, such as matrices, vectors, and eigenvalues, are introduced as essential mathematical tools for understanding machine learning algorithms.
- The unit also covers fundamental concepts like **learning from observations**, where models improve based on data patterns while balancing **bias and variance** to prevent underfitting or overfitting. The **Occam's Razor principle** is introduced, advocating for simpler models that generalize well. Furthermore, **inductive learning** and **generalization error estimation** are discussed to evaluate model performance. Lastly, the unit introduces **evaluation metrics**, including accuracy, precision, recall, and F1-score, which help assess the effectiveness of machine learning models. This foundational knowledge sets the stage for more advanced topics in applied machine learning.

## EXERCISE

### 2-Mark Questions

1. Define machine learning and its significance in real-world applications.
2. List the different types of data representations used in machine learning.
3. Differentiate between bias and variance in machine learning models.
4. State the Occam's Razor principle and its role in model selection.
5. What are the primary forms of learning in applied machine learning?
6. Mention any two applications of intelligent machines in different industries.
7. What is the importance of linear algebra in machine learning?
8. Explain the concept of generalization error in machine learning.
9. Give an example of how inductive learning is used in predictive modeling.
10. Identify two key evaluation metrics used in machine learning model assessment.

## 16 -Mark Questions

1. Analyze the role of intelligent machines in decision-making processes. How do they improve efficiency across different industries?
2. Compare and contrast different data representation techniques and discuss their impact on machine learning model performance.
3. Illustrate the various forms of learning in machine learning with examples. Explain how each form is applied in real-world scenarios.
4. Explain in detail the importance of linear algebra in machine learning. Discuss concepts such as vectors, matrices, and eigenvalues in model computations.
5. Critically evaluate the Occam's Razor principle in machine learning. Discuss how simplicity affects model performance and generalization.
6. Discuss bias-variance trade-off in machine learning models. Provide strategies to achieve a balance between underfitting and overfitting.
7. Apply the concept of inductive learning to a real-world problem. Design a learning approach based on observations and generalization.
8. Evaluate different generalization error estimation techniques. How do these techniques help in improving model accuracy?
9. Design a case study where multiple learning metrics are applied to assess a machine learning model. Justify the choice of each metric.
10. Investigate the impact of different learning paradigms in applied machine learning. How does the selection of a learning type affect problem-solving strategies?

❖❖❖

Unit 2

# Statistical Analysis in Applied Machine Learning

## Rationale

Statistical analysis plays a crucial role in machine learning, providing the foundation for data-driven decision-making and model evaluation. This unit introduces key statistical concepts essential for understanding how machine learning models interpret data, make predictions, and assess their reliability. Without a strong statistical framework, machine learning models may fail to generalize well, leading to inaccurate predictions and unreliable results.

The unit begins with an introduction to statistical analysis in machine learning, explaining its significance in extracting meaningful patterns from data. Probability theory is then explored as a fundamental tool for modeling uncertainty, enabling algorithms to make probabilistic predictions and assess confidence levels. Sampling methods are covered to highlight techniques for selecting representative data subsets, ensuring that models are trained on diverse and unbiased data. Lastly, the unit delves into inferential statistics, which helps in model validation by assessing performance metrics, confidence intervals, and hypothesis testing. These concepts are essential for ensuring robust, data-driven machine learning solutions that can perform well in real-world applications.

## 2.1 INTRODUCTION TO STATISTICAL ANALYSIS IN MACHINE LEARNING

Statistical analysis involves understanding and interpreting data patterns, variability, and relationships between variables. In machine learning, statistical methods help understand how data behaves, and they provide the foundation for many algorithms, including regression, classification, and clustering. Without a solid statistical foundation, machine learning models may overfit, underfit, or produce unreliable results.

Statistical analysis in applied machine learning is crucial for extracting meaningful insights from data and making accurate predictions. By using statistical methods, machine learning models can be built, validated, and evaluated effectively. Below is an in-depth exploration of the relationship between statistical analysis and machine learning,

### Descriptive Statistics and Data Exploration

Descriptive statistics summarize the main features of a dataset. Common tools include measures like the mean, median, mode, standard deviation, and variance. Data exploration is essential in machine learning as it helps to identify outliers, missing values, and the distribution of data, which directly influences model performance.

In applied machine learning, **descriptive statistics** and **data exploration** are essential steps to understand the dataset before building any predictive models. These techniques help in summarizing and interpreting the data, revealing important patterns, and guiding the decisions for data preprocessing, feature engineering, and model selection.

## A. Descriptive Statistics

Descriptive statistics refers to the methods used to summarize or describe the main features of a dataset. It involves measures of central tendency, variability, and the distribution of data.

Key techniques include:

### *1. Measures of Central Tendency*

- **Mean**: The average value of a dataset. For example, if you're predicting house prices, the mean might tell you the average price across all houses in your dataset.
- **Median**: The middle value when the data is sorted. It's especially useful when the data is skewed because it's less sensitive to outliers than the mean.
- **Mode**: The most frequently occurring value in the dataset. For example, in a dataset of customer ratings, the mode would identify the most common rating.

### *2. Measures of Dispersion*

- **Variance**: Measures how spread out the values are around the mean.
- **Standard Deviation**: The square root of the variance, representing the average amount of deviation from the mean.
- **Range**: The difference between the maximum and minimum values in the dataset.

### *3. Other Important Metrics*

- **Skewness**: Measures the asymmetry of the data distribution. A positive skew means more data points are on the left, while a negative skew means more data points are on the right.
- **Kurtosis**: Measures the "tailedness" of the data distribution, indicating whether the data has more extreme outliers than a normal distribution.

## B. Data Exploration

Data exploration, or **exploratory data analysis (EDA)**, involves visually and statistically examining the dataset to uncover underlying patterns, detect anomalies, and test hypotheses. Key steps in data exploration include:

### *1. Data Visualization*

- **Histograms**: Used to visualize the distribution of a single variable (e.g., the distribution of house prices).
- **Box Plots**: Useful for visualizing the spread and identifying outliers in the data. For instance, a box plot of income might reveal extreme values that need to be addressed.

- **Scatter Plots**: Helps in identifying relationships between two continuous variables. For example, plotting years of experience against salary can reveal a potential positive correlation.

## 2. Identifying Missing Values

In real-world datasets, missing values are common. EDA helps identify which variables have missing data, how much data is missing, and whether the missing data is random or follows a pattern (missing at random vs. missing not at random). For example, if the "age" field in a dataset has missing values, EDA might indicate whether imputation or deletion is the best approach.

## 3. Outlier Detection

During EDA, identifying outliers or extreme values is important, as they may distort statistical analyses and machine learning models. For example, a very high salary value in a dataset may need to be investigated or removed if it's unrealistic for the population.

## 4. Correlation Analysis

EDA often includes calculating the correlation matrix, which shows how different features relate to each other. For example, in a dataset of car prices, you might find a strong correlation between the "engine size" and "price," suggesting that engine size is an important predictor of price.

**Example:** Imagine you have a dataset of **student scores** for an exam, with columns like "age", "study hours", and "score".

## Descriptive Statistics

- The **mean score** might be 75%, suggesting that on average, students perform moderately well.
- The **median age** of the students might be 20, which could indicate that the dataset is made up mostly of young students.
- The **standard deviation of study hours** might be 10 hours, showing that most students studied within 5-15 hours, but some students studied much more or less.

## Data Exploration

- A **scatter plot** between "study hours" and "score" may show a positive correlation, suggesting that more study hours lead to higher scores.
- A **box plot** of "score" might reveal some outliers—perhaps one student scored significantly lower than the others, which could be due to errors in data entry or a rare condition.
- A **histogram** of "study hours" might show a skewed distribution, indicating that most students studied for fewer hours, but a few students studied intensively.

By combining descriptive statistics and data exploration, you get a clearer understanding of the dataset's structure, potential problems (like outliers and missing values), and patterns that inform model-building decisions, such as feature selection or pre-processing steps. This phase is crucial for ensuring that the machine learning models are built on a solid foundation.

## 2.2 PROBABILITY THEORY AND MACHINE LEARNING

Probability theory is a cornerstone of machine learning. Concepts like random variables, probability distributions, and Bayes' theorem guide how algorithms model uncertainty and predict outcomes. For instance, probabilistic models such as Naive Bayes are built on fundamental probability principles.

In applied machine learning, **probability theory** plays a central role in understanding uncertainty, making predictions, and modeling relationships between variables. Machine learning algorithms often rely on probability to make decisions about data, estimate likelihoods, and optimize models. Below is an explanation of how probability theory is applied in machine learning, along with an example.

### 1. Role of Probability Theory in Machine Learning

Probability theory provides a framework for reasoning about uncertainty. In machine learning, we often deal with uncertainty regarding outcomes (such as predicting whether an email is spam or not) or the relationships between features and the target variable. Machine learning models, especially probabilistic models, are built to estimate these uncertainties and provide predictions with a certain degree of confidence.

Key aspects where probability theory is applied in machine learning include:

- **Modeling uncertainty**: Determining how likely it is for an event to occur, given certain evidence.
- **Making predictions**: Estimating the likelihood of various possible outcomes based on available data.
- **Learning from data**: Using observed data to update and refine probability distributions.

### 2. Conditional Probability and Bayes' Theorem

One of the most fundamental applications of probability theory in machine learning is through **Bayes' Theorem**, which is used in **Bayesian inference**. Bayes' Theorem describes how to update the probability of a hypothesis based on new evidence.

Bayes' Theorem is expressed as:

$$P(H|E) = \{ P(E|H).P(H)\} / P(E)$$

Where:

- P(H|E)P(H|E) is the **posterior probability** (the probability of the hypothesis HH given the evidence EE).
- P(E|H)P(E|H) is the **likelihood** (the probability of observing the evidence EE given the hypothesis HH).
- P(H)P(H) is the **prior probability** (the initial probability of the hypothesis before observing evidence).
- P(E)P(E) is the **evidence** (the total probability of the evidence under all hypotheses).

This theorem is crucial in machine learning for tasks like classification, especially in models like **Naive Bayes**.

## 3. Naive Bayes Classifier Example

Naive Bayes is a simple, yet powerful probabilistic classification model based on Bayes' Theorem. It assumes that the features in the dataset are conditionally independent given the target class (this is the "naive" assumption).

**Example**: Consider a binary classification problem where we want to predict whether an email is spam or not based on the words it contains. The features could be the presence or absence of certain words (e.g., "buy", "now", "limited offer").

- **Training Data**: We have a labeled dataset with emails marked as either "spam" or "not spam".
- **Bayes' Theorem**: Using Bayes' Theorem, we can compute the probability of an email being spam given certain words are present in the email. For example, if the words "buy" and "now" appear in an email, we calculate the likelihood of the email being spam, given these words.

The model calculates the likelihood of each word given the class (spam or not spam) and the prior probability of spam vs. non-spam emails. By comparing these probabilities for both classes, the model classifies the email as spam or not spam.

## 4. Maximum Likelihood Estimation (MLE)

In machine learning, **Maximum Likelihood Estimation (MLE)** is used to estimate the parameters of a probabilistic model. It seeks to find the parameter values that maximize the likelihood of the observed data.

## 5. Probabilistic Models for Classification and Regression

Many machine learning models are inherently probabilistic, such as:

- **Logistic Regression**: A classification algorithm that predicts the probability of a binary outcome. It uses a logistic function to model the probability of a class given the input features. The output is a value between 0 and 1, which can be interpreted as the likelihood of an instance belonging to the positive class.
- **Gaussian Naive Bayes**: In cases where the features are continuous, a Gaussian distribution is assumed for each feature in a class. The model calculates the likelihood of a feature under the assumption of normality and uses Bayes' Theorem to classify instances.
- **Gaussian Mixture Models (GMM)**: These are generative probabilistic models that assume the data is generated from a mixture of several Gaussian distributions. They are useful for clustering tasks where the data is assumed to come from multiple subpopulations.

## 6. Markov Chains and Hidden Markov Models

In sequential data, such as time series or natural language processing (NLP), **Markov Chains** and **Hidden Markov Models (HMM)** are widely used probabilistic models. A Markov Chain is a random process where the future state depends only on the current state, not the previous states. HMMs are used when the system being modeled has unobservable (hidden) states, such as in speech recognition or part-of-speech tagging.

**Example:** In speech recognition, the HMM may model the probability of certain phonemes (the hidden states) given the observed sound signals (the visible states). The model is trained to learn the transitions between phonemes and their corresponding sound features.

### 7. Monte Carlo Methods and Probabilistic Inference

Monte Carlo methods, including **Markov Chain Monte Carlo (MCMC)**, are used in probabilistic machine learning for approximating complex probability distributions. These methods generate samples from the target distribution and use these samples to estimate expectations and other quantities.

**Example:** In **Bayesian deep learning**, MCMC methods can be used to approximate the posterior distribution of the weights in a neural network. This allows the model to account for uncertainty in the model's predictions, providing a range of potential outcomes instead of a single deterministic prediction.

Probability theory in machine learning allows models to reason about uncertainty, make predictions, and improve learning from data. Techniques such as Bayes' Theorem, Maximum Likelihood Estimation, and probabilistic models like Naive Bayes and Logistic Regression are essential in many applied machine learning tasks. These methods help to quantify uncertainty, make informed predictions, and optimize models in uncertain environments, which are key in real-world machine learning applications.

## 2.3 SAMPLING METHODS

In applied machine learning, sampling methods like random sampling, stratified sampling, and bootstrapping are used to create subsets of data for training and testing. These methods ensure that models generalize well and do not overfit to particular subsets of the data.

Sampling methods are fundamental in applied machine learning, as they allow us to create representative subsets of data from a larger dataset, which are then used to train and evaluate models. These techniques ensure that the model generalizes well and avoids issues such as overfitting or bias. Below are seven key aspects of sampling methods in machine learning, with examples for each.

### 1. Importance of Sampling in Machine Learning

In machine learning, collecting and working with the entire dataset may not always be feasible due to time or resource constraints. Sampling methods help mitigate these issues by selecting smaller, manageable subsets of the data that still reflect the underlying patterns of the whole dataset. Proper sampling ensures that machine learning models are trained on diverse, representative data, improving their ability to generalize to new, unseen data.

For example, in a customer churn prediction model, the dataset may contain millions of records. Instead of training the model on the entire dataset, which might be computationally expensive, sampling methods can select a representative subset to train the model efficiently without losing predictive power.

### 2. Random Sampling

Random sampling is the simplest and most commonly used sampling method. It involves selecting a random subset of data points from the entire dataset, where each data point has an equal chance of being chosen. This method is effective when the dataset is homogeneous and each sample is independent.

For example, if you are building a predictive model for house prices, random sampling could involve selecting a subset of houses from different neighborhoods, without bias towards any specific area, to create a training dataset. Random sampling helps avoid biases in the data, but it might not always capture important trends, especially if the data is imbalanced.

### 3. Stratified Sampling

Stratified sampling is used when the dataset has distinct subgroups, or **strata**, and it's important to ensure that each subgroup is adequately represented in the sample. In this method, the data is divided into different strata (subgroups based on a particular feature), and random samples are drawn from each group proportionally or equally.

For instance, in a binary classification problem where the classes are imbalanced (e.g., 95% non-churn and 5% churn in a customer churn prediction model), using random sampling may result in a model that doesn't learn to predict the minority class well. Stratified sampling ensures that both churn and non-churn customers are well-represented in the training set, allowing the model to learn from both classes effectively.

### 4. Systematic Sampling

Systematic sampling involves selecting every *k*th data point from an ordered dataset. This approach can be more efficient than simple random sampling, especially when the dataset is ordered in some way (such as time-series data). The choice of *k* determines the sample size.

For example, if you have a time-series dataset of daily stock prices and you want to train a model on every 10th day's data, you would use systematic sampling. However, care must be taken when the data has an underlying periodicity. If the data is ordered in such a way that there's a pattern or seasonality (e.g., daily stock prices following a weekly trend), systematic sampling may lead to bias in the sample.

### 5. Bootstrap Sampling

Bootstrap sampling is a technique used to create multiple training datasets by randomly sampling with replacement from the original dataset. In this method, some data points may appear multiple times in the sample, while others may not appear at all. It is especially useful in ensemble methods like bagging (e.g., Random Forest) to create diverse models and reduce variance.

An example would be in a random forest model, where multiple decision trees are trained on different bootstrap samples of the data. By combining the predictions of all these trees, the model becomes more robust and accurate than if it were based on a single training set. Bootstrap sampling is beneficial for creating a variety of models, as each sample is slightly different.

### 6. Leave-One-Out Sampling (LOO)

Leave-One-Out Sampling (LOO) is a special case of cross-validation, where the dataset is split such that each sample in the dataset is used once as the validation set while the remaining samples are used for training. This method is particularly useful when you have a small dataset and want to maximize the training data for every model evaluation.

For example, in a small dataset of 10 images for object classification, you would train the model 10 times, each time leaving out one image for validation. The main advantage of

LOO is that it uses every available data point for both training and testing, making it useful when data is scarce. However, it can be computationally expensive for large datasets.

### 7. Oversampling and Undersampling

Oversampling and undersampling are techniques used to handle **imbalanced datasets**, where one class is underrepresented compared to another. **Oversampling** involves duplicating samples from the minority class to balance the dataset, while **undersampling** involves reducing the number of samples from the majority class.

For example, in a fraud detection model, if only 1% of transactions are fraudulent, the model may be biased toward predicting "non-fraud" because of the imbalance. By oversampling the fraudulent transactions or undersampling the non-fraudulent ones, you create a more balanced dataset that allows the model to learn to identify fraudulent transactions more accurately. However, oversampling can lead to overfitting, while undersampling may result in losing valuable information.

Sampling methods in applied machine learning are crucial for selecting representative subsets of data, ensuring that models are trained efficiently and generalize well. Techniques like random sampling, stratified sampling, and bootstrap sampling help address issues like data imbalance, overfitting, and computational constraints. Each method has its strengths and weaknesses, and the choice of sampling technique depends on the nature of the data and the specific machine learning task at hand. Proper sampling ensures that the model is robust, unbiased, and capable of making accurate predictions on new, unseen data.

## 2.4 INFERENTIAL STATISTICS IN MODEL VALIDATION

Inferential statistics help make conclusions about a population based on sample data. In machine learning, inferential methods are used to validate model performance, such as hypothesis testing (e.g., t-tests) to assess whether model improvements are statistically significant.

**Inferential statistics** plays a crucial role in model validation within applied machine learning. It involves making generalizations about a population based on a sample of data, helping to assess whether a model's performance or findings are statistically significant, or if the results could have occurred by chance.

In machine learning, inferential statistics provides the foundation for hypothesis testing, confidence intervals, and the evaluation of model parameters. Below is a detailed explanation with an example in seven paragraphs.

### 1. Overview of Inferential Statistics in Model Validation

In machine learning, inferential statistics is used to validate whether the model's performance or its predictions are reliable and applicable to the broader population. It allows us to estimate the precision and reliability of model parameters, assess whether observed improvements in performance are statistically significant, and evaluate the model's generalizability beyond the training data. Unlike descriptive statistics, which merely summarize the data, inferential statistics allows us to make inferences or predictions based on the data.

### 2. Hypothesis Testing

One key application of inferential statistics in model validation is hypothesis testing. This process helps determine if a particular observation or result is statistically significant. For example, when comparing two models to see which performs better, hypothesis testing can be used to test whether the difference in performance is significant or just due to random variation. The null hypothesis ($H_0$) typically assumes no effect or difference, while the alternative hypothesis ($H_1$) suggests that the models do differ in performance.

**Example**: Suppose we are comparing the performance of two machine learning models (e.g., a decision tree and a logistic regression) on a classification task. A hypothesis test (like a t-test or ANOVA) can be used to determine if the difference in their accuracies is statistically significant. If the p-value is low (typically below 0.05), we can reject the null hypothesis and conclude that the difference is likely not due to chance.

## 3. Confidence Intervals

Another important inferential statistic used in model validation is **confidence intervals (CIs)**. A confidence interval provides a range of values within which we can be reasonably confident that the true model performance or parameter lies.

For example, instead of just reporting a model's accuracy as a point estimate (say 85%), a confidence interval could be used to express the uncertainty around this estimate (e.g., the accuracy is between 82% and 88% with 95% confidence).

**Example**: After training a regression model, you may want to estimate the confidence interval for the model's coefficient for a particular feature. This interval provides insight into how certain the model is about the contribution of that feature. If the confidence interval for the coefficient includes zero, it might suggest that the feature is not statistically significant in predicting the target.

## 4. Cross-Validation and Bias-Variance Tradeoff

Inferential statistics is crucial in model validation methods such as **cross-validation**, which helps assess how a model generalizes to unseen data. Cross-validation splits the data into several subsets (folds), where the model is trained on some folds and tested on the remaining ones. By using inferential statistics, we can calculate the confidence intervals for performance metrics (e.g., accuracy, F1 score) obtained during cross-validation, helping us to understand how much variation exists in model performance.

**Example:** In k-fold cross-validation, the performance metric is computed for each fold, and inferential statistics can be used to determine the variability across folds. A large variation in performance metrics across folds could suggest that the model is overfitting or sensitive to the specific data partition.

## 5. Evaluating Model Parameters

In many machine learning models, such as linear regression or logistic regression, inferential statistics helps evaluate the significance of model parameters. By examining the p-values and confidence intervals for the model's coefficients, we can assess whether each feature contributes meaningfully to the model's predictions. This allows for better interpretability and the possibility of improving model performance by removing irrelevant features.

**Example**: In linear regression, after fitting the model, each coefficient will have an associated p-value. If the p-value for a particular coefficient is high (typically greater than 0.05), it suggests that the feature corresponding to that coefficient might not have a significant relationship with the target variable. In this case, you might consider removing the feature from the model to simplify it and avoid overfitting.

## 6. Model Comparison using Statistical Tests

When comparing multiple machine learning models, inferential statistics provides a framework for determining whether the differences in performance are statistically significant. Common statistical tests include the paired t-test, McNemar's test, and ANOVA, each of which helps to assess if the performance difference between models is due to random chance or reflects real, meaningful differences.

**Example**: Suppose you have two models: Model A (a neural network) and Model B (a decision tree) for predicting customer churn. To compare their performances, you can use a **paired t-test** to see if the difference in their accuracies is statistically significant. The test would evaluate whether the improvement in performance with Model A is greater than what could be expected due to random variation, providing confidence in your choice of the better model.

## 7. Limitations of Inferential Statistics in Machine Learning

While inferential statistics is powerful for model validation, it has limitations in machine learning. For example, traditional hypothesis tests assume that the data is independent and identically distributed (i.i.d.), which may not always be the case in machine learning datasets, especially in time-series or spatial data.

Moreover, in complex models like deep learning, the relationships between features and target variables may not be easily interpretable using traditional inferential techniques. In such cases, advanced methods like bootstrapping or Bayesian inference might be required.

**Example**: If you're working with time-series data for predicting stock prices, inferential statistics like hypothesis testing may not be applicable, as time-series data is often autocorrelated (previous observations affect future ones). In such cases, techniques like cross-validation for time-series or Bayesian models can be more appropriate for validating the model.

Inferential statistics is a vital tool in machine learning model validation. It helps us assess whether the model's performance or parameter estimates are reliable, determine if improvements in performance are statistically significant, and estimate the uncertainty around predictions.

Through methods like hypothesis testing, confidence intervals, and model comparison tests, inferential statistics allows practitioners to make data-driven decisions with confidence. However, it's essential to be aware of its limitations and the assumptions behind these techniques to apply them effectively in machine learning contexts.

# STATISTICAL ANALYSIS AND ITS ROLE IN APPLIED MACHINE LEARNING

Statistical analysis serves as the foundation of applied machine learning, enabling practitioners to explore, interpret, and validate data effectively. It provides the framework for understanding relationships among variables, selecting relevant features, evaluating model performance, and ensuring reliability in predictions.

From simple correlations to complex inference techniques, statistical principles guide every stage of model development. The following key aspects illustrate how statistical analysis strengthens the machine learning process:

## 1. Correlation and Causation

Understanding relationships between variables is key in machine learning. Correlation measures the strength and direction of linear relationships between features, while causation refers to cause-and-effect relationships. While correlation can guide feature selection, causality requires more advanced techniques and careful design of experiments.

## 2. Linear Regression and Statistical Significance

Linear regression is one of the simplest machine learning models. It involves predicting a target variable as a linear function of input features. Statistical significance tests, such as p-values, are used to assess whether the relationships between features and the target variable are meaningful.

## 3. Multivariate Analysis and Feature Selection

Multivariate analysis explores the relationship between multiple variables simultaneously. In machine learning, multivariate statistical techniques, such as principal component analysis (PCA) or multiple regression, are used for feature selection and dimensionality reduction to improve model efficiency and accuracy.

## 4. Hypothesis Testing in Machine Learning

Hypothesis testing is used to determine whether a model's performance improvement is due to the implemented changes or just random chance. For example, comparing two models' accuracy using tests like the chi-square test or ANOVA can help determine if one model significantly outperforms another.

## 5. Bayesian Inference in Machine Learning

Bayesian inference is a statistical technique that updates the probability of a hypothesis based on new data. In machine learning, Bayesian methods, like Bayesian networks or Bayesian optimization, provide a framework for model selection, hyperparameter tuning, and uncertainty quantification.

## 6. Overfitting, Underfitting, and Bias-Variance Tradeoff

Statistical analysis helps identify and address overfitting and underfitting issues in machine learning. Overfitting occurs when a model learns too much from the training data, while underfitting happens when the model fails to capture the underlying data patterns. The bias-variance tradeoff highlights the balance between the two extremes, guiding model complexity.

## 7. Cross-Validation Techniques

Cross-validation is a statistical method used to assess the generalization performance of a model. By splitting the dataset into multiple folds, cross-validation ensures that the model's performance is robust and not overly dependent on any single subset of data. Common techniques include k-fold cross-validation and leave-one-out cross-validation.

## 8. Confusion Matrix and Evaluation Metrics

The confusion matrix is a key statistical tool for evaluating classification models. It provides counts of true positives, false positives, true negatives, and false negatives. From the confusion matrix, various performance metrics like accuracy, precision, recall, F1 score, and AUC-ROC can be derived.

## 9. Statistical Learning Theory

Statistical learning theory provides the foundation for understanding the behavior of machine learning algorithms. It helps in analyzing the performance of algorithms, offering insights into their capacity for generalization, and explaining the bias-variance tradeoff, capacity control, and error rates in a mathematical framework.

## 10. Error Analysis and Model Improvement

Understanding errors is essential for improving machine learning models. Statistical techniques such as residual analysis help identify patterns of bias or variance that could lead to underperformance. Error analysis involves looking at misclassified examples or predicting the most frequent errors to refine the model.

## 11. Time Series Analysis in Machine Learning

Time series data is common in many machine learning applications. Statistical techniques such as autocorrelation, moving averages, and ARIMA models are often used to analyze and forecast temporal patterns in data. These methods are vital for predicting future trends based on historical data.

## 12. Non-Parametric Methods

Non-parametric methods do not assume a specific distribution for the data, making them more flexible and widely applicable. Examples include the k-nearest neighbors (KNN) algorithm, decision trees, and the Mann-Whitney U test. These methods are useful when data does not meet the assumptions of parametric tests.

## 13. Clustering and Statistical Analysis

Clustering techniques, like k-means and hierarchical clustering, rely on statistical principles to group similar data points. These methods use distance metrics or probabilistic models to determine clusters, with statistical validation methods like silhouette scores and Dunn indices used to assess clustering quality.

## 14. Ensemble Methods and Statistical Aggregation

Ensemble methods, such as random forests and gradient boosting, combine multiple models to improve predictive accuracy. Statistical techniques like bootstrapping or bagging are used to aggregate predictions from individual models, thereby reducing variance and increasing overall performance.

## 15. The Role of Statistical Analysis in Machine Learning

Statistical analysis is indispensable in applied machine learning as it enhances the reliability and interpretability of models. From data exploration and model validation to feature selection and error analysis, statistical methods guide the entire machine learning process. As machine learning continues to evolve, integrating advanced statistical techniques will be key to building accurate, robust, and trustworthy models.

Through these steps, statistical analysis informs decision-making, enhances model performance, and ensures that machine learning models are grounded in solid, reliable data.

## UNIT SUMMARY

- This unit explores the critical role of **statistical analysis** in applied machine learning, providing the foundation for data-driven decision-making. The introduction highlights how statistical techniques support model development, ensuring reliability and accuracy in predictions. Statistical methods help in understanding data distributions, identifying patterns, and assessing model performance, making them indispensable in the field of machine learning.
- A key component of this unit is **probability theory**, which serves as the backbone of many machine learning algorithms. Concepts such as probability distributions, Bayes' theorem, and conditional probabilities are examined to demonstrate their applications in predictive modeling and classification tasks. The unit also covers **sampling methods**, which are essential for handling large datasets efficiently. Techniques like random sampling, stratified sampling, and bootstrapping help improve model generalization while minimizing bias.
- Another crucial aspect discussed is **inferential statistics**, which plays a vital role in model validation. Hypothesis testing, confidence intervals, and p-values are explored to assess the statistical significance of machine learning results. These methods ensure that models are not only accurate on training data but also perform well on unseen data. By integrating statistical principles with machine learning, this unit equips learners with the tools necessary to build robust and interpretable models for real-world applications.

## EXERCISE

### 2-Mark Questions

1. Define statistical analysis in the context of machine learning.
2. What is the role of probability theory in machine learning?
3. Differentiate between descriptive and inferential statistics.
4. What is a probability distribution? Give an example.
5. List two commonly used sampling methods in machine learning.
6. What is the importance of hypothesis testing in model validation?
7. Define overfitting and explain how statistical methods help in preventing it.
8. What is p-value in statistical inference?
9. Explain the significance of confidence intervals in model evaluation.
10. What is the central limit theorem and why is it important in machine learning?

### 16 -Mark Questions

1. Explain the significance of statistical analysis in machine learning with suitable examples.
2. Discuss in detail the role of probability theory in machine learning, including Bayes' Theorem and its applications.
3. Analyze different types of probability distributions (Normal, Binomial, Poisson) and their impact on machine learning models.

4. Compare and contrast different sampling methods such as random sampling, stratified sampling, and bootstrapping in machine learning.
5. Explain inferential statistics and discuss how it is applied in model validation with real-world examples.
6. Discuss the bias-variance tradeoff in statistical learning and suggest ways to achieve a balance.
7. Evaluate different hypothesis testing techniques used in statistical model validation and their importance in predictive analytics.
8. Explain various statistical metrics (such as RMSE, $R^2$, and MAE) used for model evaluation in machine learning.
9. How does statistical significance impact the reliability of machine learning models? Support your answer with appropriate examples.
10. Design a case study where statistical analysis plays a crucial role in improving the performance of a machine learning model.

*Unit* **3**

# Introduction to Neural Networks

## Rationale

Neural networks are the backbone of modern artificial intelligence and deep learning, enabling machines to learn and make complex decisions. This unit is designed to provide a foundational understanding of neural network principles, their evolution, and their role in solving real-world problems. By studying neural networks, learners can grasp how machines recognize patterns, process information, and improve performance over time, which is essential for applications like image recognition, speech processing, and financial forecasting.

The unit begins with the characteristics of neural networks, explaining their ability to model non-linear relationships and learn from large datasets. It then explores the historical development of neural networks, tracing key advancements from early perceptron models to deep learning breakthroughs. The discussion of Artificial Neural Networks (ANNs) introduces fundamental components such as neurons, activation functions, and learning algorithms, which form the basis of modern AI models. Lastly, the Feedforward Neural Networks (FNNs) section explains the simplest neural network architecture, where information flows in a single direction, making it essential for supervised learning tasks. This unit builds a strong conceptual framework for understanding advanced neural architectures and their applications.

## 3.1 CHARACTERISTICS OF NEURAL NETWORKS

### 1. Definition of Neural Networks

Neural networks are computational models inspired by the way biological neural networks in the human brain function. They consist of layers of interconnected nodes (or "neurons") that process information in complex ways. Neural networks can learn from data, generalize from patterns, and make decisions or predictions. They are a subset of machine learning and are widely used in tasks like classification, regression, pattern recognition, and reinforcement learning.

### 2. Structure of Neural Networks

A neural network typically consists of three layers: an input layer, one or more hidden layers, and an output layer. The input layer receives the raw data, the hidden layers process the data through neurons, and the output layer provides the final result. Each layer is made up of numerous nodes, which are mathematical functions designed to process input and pass it on to the next layer.

## 3. Neurons and Activation Functions

Each node in a neural network represents a neuron, which takes input values, applies weights, and passes them through an activation function. The activation function determines whether a neuron should be activated or not. Common activation functions include the sigmoid, tanh, ReLU (Rectified Linear Unit), and softmax functions. These functions help introduce non-linearity, enabling neural networks to learn complex patterns.

## 4. Weights and Biases

In a neural network, connections between neurons are associated with weights, which represent the strength of the relationship between neurons. During training, these weights are adjusted to minimize the error between the predicted and actual output. Additionally, each neuron has a bias term, which allows the activation function to be shifted, giving the network more flexibility in modeling data.

## 5. Forward Propagation

Forward propagation is the process by which data is passed through the layers of the network. The input features are fed into the input layer, and through the weighted connections and activation functions, the information propagates forward through the hidden layers, ultimately reaching the output layer. The output of the network is then compared to the true values, and the error is computed.

## 6. Loss Function

The loss function (or cost function) measures the difference between the predicted output and the actual output. The goal of training a neural network is to minimize this loss function. For regression tasks, Mean Squared Error (MSE) is commonly used, while for classification, Cross-Entropy loss is frequently employed. A lower loss indicates a better-performing model.

## 7. Backpropagation

Backpropagation is the process used to update the weights and biases of a neural network during training. After forward propagation, the network calculates the error, and backpropagation helps the network learn by adjusting the weights to reduce that error. It works by calculating the gradient of the loss function with respect to each weight using the chain rule of calculus and updating the weights in the opposite direction of the gradient.

## 8. Optimization and Gradient Descent

Optimization refers to the process of minimizing the loss function during training. One of the most common optimization techniques is Gradient Descent. In this method, the weights are updated iteratively by calculating the gradient of the loss function and moving in the direction that reduces the error. Variants like Stochastic Gradient Descent (SGD), Mini-batch Gradient Descent, and Adam optimize the training process further.

## 9. Learning Rate

The learning rate controls how much the weights are adjusted with each step of gradient descent. If the learning rate is too high, the network might overshoot the optimal weights, while a low learning rate may result in slow convergence. Proper tuning of the learning rate is crucial for effective training.

## 10. Overfitting and Underfitting

Overfitting occurs when a neural network learns the training data too well, including noise or irrelevant patterns, resulting in poor generalization to new data. Underfitting happens when the model is too simple to capture the underlying data patterns. Techniques such as dropout, regularization, and early stopping are used to prevent overfitting and achieve the right balance between bias and variance.

## 11. Types of Neural Networks

There are various types of neural networks designed for specific tasks. Some of the common types include:

- **Feedforward Neural Networks (FNN):** The simplest form of neural networks where information moves in one direction, from input to output.
- **Convolutional Neural Networks (CNN):** Specialized for image processing, these networks use convolutional layers to automatically extract features from images.
- **Recurrent Neural Networks (RNN):** Designed for sequential data, RNNs have loops in their structure, allowing them to retain information from previous time steps.
- **Generative Adversarial Networks (GAN):** Used for generating new data, such as images, by pitting two networks against each other in a game-like scenario.

## 12. Deep Learning

Deep learning refers to neural networks with many hidden layers, often termed as "deep neural networks." The increased depth allows these networks to learn hierarchical representations of data, making them suitable for complex tasks such as speech recognition, natural language processing, and autonomous driving. The use of multiple layers helps the network capture abstract features and make decisions based on higher-level representations.

## 13. Training Data and Batch Processing

The performance of neural networks heavily depends on the quality and quantity of the training data. A large, diverse dataset helps the model generalize well. To optimize the training process, data is often processed in batches rather than all at once, which improves computational efficiency and helps avoid local minima. Batch training can also be used in conjunction with techniques like Mini-batch Gradient Descent.

## 14. Regularization Techniques

Regularization techniques are applied to prevent overfitting and improve the generalization of the neural network. Popular regularization methods include:

- **L1 and L2 Regularization:** These methods add penalties to the loss function based on the magnitude of the weights, discouraging large weights that could lead to overfitting.
- **Dropout:** This technique randomly "drops" certain neurons during training to prevent the network from relying too heavily on specific nodes, enhancing generalization.
- **Early Stopping:** Monitoring the model's performance on a validation set and stopping training when performance starts to degrade helps prevent overfitting.

## 15. Transfer Learning

Transfer learning is a technique where a pre-trained model is adapted to solve a new, related problem. This is especially useful when the amount of available data for a new task is limited. The lower layers of the pre-trained model, which typically capture general features, can be reused, while only the higher layers need to be retrained for the new task.

## 16. Applications of Neural Networks

Neural networks have a wide range of applications across various fields, including:

- **Image Recognition:** Used in facial recognition, object detection, and medical imaging.
- **Natural Language Processing:** Neural networks are employed in language translation, speech recognition, and chatbots.
- **Autonomous Systems:** Used in self-driving cars and robotics for decision-making.
- **Finance and Healthcare:** Employed for fraud detection, stock prediction, and disease diagnosis. The versatility of neural networks continues to drive advancements in artificial intelligence and machine learning.

# 3.2 HISTORICAL DEVELOPMENT OF NEURAL NETWORKS PRINCIPLES

## 1. Early Foundations of Neural Networks

The historical development of neural networks can be traced back to the mid-20th century, with early concepts rooted in biological neural systems. The idea that machines could simulate the brain's processing mechanisms gained traction through the work of researchers who sought to understand how humans process information. The initial inspiration came from the structure of biological neurons, which led to the development of mathematical models designed to mimic these processes.

## 2. The McCulloch-Pitts Model (1943)

In 1943, Warren McCulloch and Walter Pitts introduced the first conceptual model of an artificial neuron, known as the McCulloch-Pitts model. This model represented neurons as simple logical functions, where each neuron could either "fire" or remain inactive depending on its inputs. The model was based on binary logic, and it laid the foundation for later developments in neural networks by introducing the concept of a threshold for neuron activation and weighted inputs.

## 3. Hebbian Learning (1949)

Donald Hebb's 1949 work on learning in the brain led to the development of the Hebbian learning rule, which proposed that connections between neurons strengthen when they are activated simultaneously. This principle, often summarized as "cells that fire together wire together," became a fundamental idea in neural network learning, influencing later models like the perceptron and more complex systems that incorporated learning based on input-output patterns.

## 4. The Perceptron (1958)

In 1958, Frank Rosenblatt developed the perceptron, one of the earliest neural network models. It was a simple, single-layer neural network designed for binary classification tasks. The perceptron could learn from data by adjusting the weights associated with its input features using the perceptron learning rule, which is a form of supervised learning. While limited to linear separability, the perceptron marked a milestone in neural network history by demonstrating that machines could "learn" from data.

## 5. Perceptron Limitations and the AI Winter (1960s-1970s)

Despite the initial enthusiasm surrounding the perceptron, its limitations became clear in the 1960s. One of the most significant challenges was its inability to solve problems that were not linearly separable, such as the XOR problem. In 1969, Marvin Minsky and Seymour Papert published *Perceptrons*, a book that highlighted the theoretical and practical shortcomings of the perceptron model. This led to a decline in interest and funding for neural network research, resulting in the so-called "AI Winter," a period of stagnation in artificial intelligence development during the 1970s.

## 6. Backpropagation and Multi-Layer Networks (1980s)

The revival of neural networks came in the 1980s with the rediscovery of backpropagation, a key algorithm for training multi-layer networks. Backpropagation, first introduced by Paul Werbos in 1974 and popularized by Geoffrey Hinton, David Rumelhart, and Ronald Williams in 1986, allowed neural networks to update weights through the gradient descent method. This enabled training of deep networks with multiple hidden layers, solving the issue of non-linear separability and opening the door for more complex models capable of solving a wider range of tasks.

## 7. The Rise of Deep Learning (1990s-2000s)

In the 1990s and 2000s, deep learning began to take shape as advancements in computational power and data availability facilitated the training of more sophisticated models. During this period, researchers started developing deeper neural networks with more hidden layers, known as deep neural networks (DNNs). However, the training of deep networks was still challenging due to issues like vanishing gradients, which limited their practical use.

## 8. Convolutional Neural Networks (CNNs) and Computer Vision (1989-2012)

Convolutional Neural Networks (CNNs) were introduced by Yann LeCun in the late 1980s, and their breakthrough came in 2012 with the success of AlexNet, a CNN architecture that won the ImageNet competition by a significant margin. AlexNet demonstrated the power of

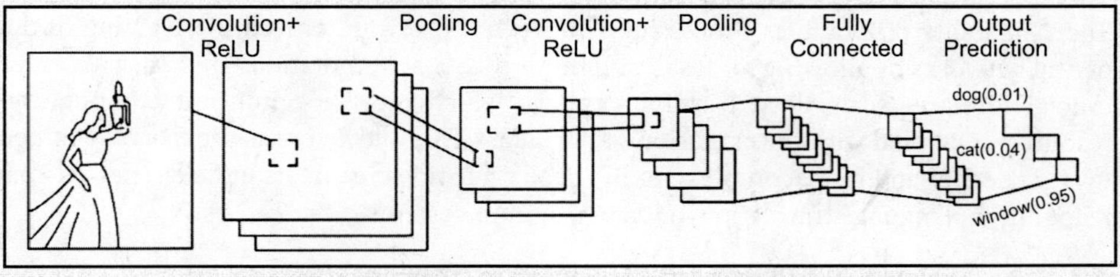


***Fig 3.1** Working Procedure of CNN*

*Figure 3.1 shows the working procedure of CNN.*

deep learning for image recognition tasks. The success of CNNs marked a turning point in neural network research, making them the go-to model for computer vision tasks.

## 9. Recurrent Neural Networks (RNNs) and Sequence Modeling (1980s-Present)

Recurrent Neural Networks (RNNs), first introduced by John Hopfield in the 1980s and further developed by others, were designed to handle sequential data by incorporating loops in the network. This architecture allows RNNs to retain memory of previous inputs, making them ideal for tasks such as language modeling, speech recognition, and time-series analysis. However, traditional RNNs faced challenges with long-term dependencies, which were addressed later by architectures like Long Short-Term Memory (LSTM) networks.

## 10. The LSTM Breakthrough (1997)

In 1997, Sepp Hochreiter and Jürgen Schmidhuber introduced the Long Short-Term Memory (LSTM) network, a specific type of RNN that addresses the vanishing gradient problem. LSTMs incorporate memory cells that can retain information for long periods, allowing them to model long-range dependencies in sequences. This breakthrough made LSTMs a powerful tool for natural language processing (NLP), machine translation, and speech recognition, among other tasks.

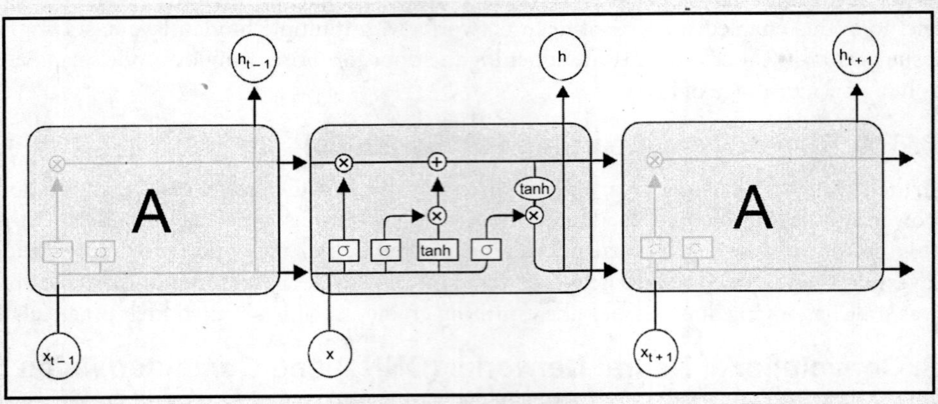


*Fig.3.2 Working Procedure of LSTM*

*Figure.3.2 shows the working procedure of LSTM.*

## 11. GPU Acceleration and Big Data (2000s-Present)

The availability of Graphics Processing Units (GPUs) revolutionized the training of deep neural networks by allowing for faster and more efficient computation. This was particularly crucial for large-scale deep learning models, which require significant computational resources. Coupled with the explosion of big data, GPUs allowed researchers and engineers to train deeper and more complex models, leading to advancements in fields such as image recognition, language translation, and autonomous systems.

## 12. Generative Adversarial Networks (GANs) (2014)

In 2014, Ian Goodfellow introduced Generative Adversarial Networks (GANs), a novel approach to generative modeling. GANs consist of two networks: a generator, which creates synthetic data, and a discriminator, which evaluates the authenticity of the data. The two networks are trained in a competitive process, which leads to the generation of highly realistic data. GANs have found applications in art generation, image enhancement, and data augmentation.

### 13. Transformer Models and Attention Mechanisms (2017)

The introduction of the Transformer model in 2017 by Vaswani et al. revolutionized natural language processing tasks. The Transformer uses self-attention mechanisms to capture relationships between words in a sequence, allowing it to handle long-range dependencies more effectively than traditional RNNs and LSTMs. Transformer models have become the foundation for state-of-the-art language models like GPT, BERT, and T5, which have pushed the boundaries of NLP performance.

### 14. The Role of Open-Source Libraries (2010s-Present)

The development of open-source libraries such as TensorFlow, Keras, PyTorch, and Caffe has played a significant role in making deep learning accessible to researchers and practitioners. These libraries provide pre-built functions and tools for building, training, and deploying neural networks, enabling rapid experimentation and development. The open-source nature of these libraries has accelerated innovation and collaboration in the deep learning community.

### 15. Current Trends and the Future of Neural Networks

Today, neural networks continue to evolve, with ongoing research focusing on improving model efficiency, interpretability, and generalization. Areas such as neural architecture search, unsupervised learning, and reinforcement learning are gaining traction. Additionally, the focus is shifting towards the ethical implications of AI and ensuring that neural networks are used in ways that are transparent, fair, and beneficial to society. As computational resources continue to grow and more advanced algorithms are developed, neural networks are expected to remain at the forefront of AI research and applications.

## 3.3 ARTIFICIAL NEURAL NETWORKS

### 1. Introduction to Artificial Neural Networks (ANNs)

Artificial Neural Networks (ANNs) are computational models inspired by the structure and function of the human brain. They are designed to recognize patterns and relationships in data, making them a fundamental tool in applied machine learning. ANNs consist of interconnected nodes (neurons) organized into layers, which allow them to process complex input-output mappings. By learning from data, ANNs can make predictions, classify information, or generate new data, making them widely used in tasks like image recognition, natural language processing, and predictive analytics.

### 2. Basic Structure of an ANN

An ANN typically consists of three main layers: the input layer, hidden layers, and output layer. The input layer receives data features, which are then processed through the hidden layers before being mapped to an output. Each layer contains several neurons that are connected by weights, which determine the importance of the connections. The hidden layers enable the network to capture complex patterns and abstractions in the data, while the output layer produces the final result, such as a classification label or a numerical value.

## 3. Neurons and Activation Functions

Each neuron in an ANN receives input, processes it through a mathematical function, and produces an output. The most common activation functions used in ANNs include the sigmoid, tanh, and ReLU (Rectified Linear Unit) functions. These activation functions introduce non-linearity, allowing the network to model complex relationships in the data. For instance, ReLU is often preferred in deep learning applications because it helps mitigate the vanishing gradient problem and allows faster training.

## 4. Weights and Biases

In an ANN, each connection between neurons has a weight associated with it, and each neuron has a bias term. The weight determines the strength of the connection between neurons, while the bias allows the network to adjust the output independently of the inputs. During the training process, both the weights and biases are updated using optimization techniques to minimize the error between predicted and actual values. These updates enable the network to learn and improve its predictions over time.

## 5. Forward Propagation

Forward propagation is the process by which input data is passed through the network to generate an output. Starting from the input layer, the data is passed through the hidden layers, where each neuron performs weighted summation of inputs and applies the activation function. The output layer then produces the final result. The network's output is compared to the true output, and the error is calculated using a loss function, which quantifies the difference between the predicted and actual outputs.

## 6. Loss Function

The loss function, also known as the cost function, measures the error between the predicted output and the actual target values. In machine learning, the goal is to minimize the loss function, which indicates that the network's predictions are becoming more accurate. For classification tasks, commonly used loss functions include cross-entropy loss, while for regression tasks, mean squared error (MSE) is often used. The choice of loss function depends on the type of problem the neural network is solving.

## 7. Backpropagation and Gradient Descent

Backpropagation is the algorithm used to train ANNs by adjusting the weights and biases based on the error calculated from the output. Backpropagation computes the gradient of the loss function with respect to each weight and bias by applying the chain rule of calculus. These gradients are then used to update the parameters using an optimization algorithm, such as gradient descent. Gradient descent minimizes the loss function iteratively by adjusting the weights in the direction of the negative gradient, leading to better predictions.

## 8. Gradient Descent Variants

Standard gradient descent can be slow and computationally expensive, especially when dealing with large datasets. To address this, several variants of gradient descent have been developed, including Stochastic Gradient Descent (SGD), Mini-batch Gradient Descent, and Adam. SGD updates weights based on a single data point, making it faster but noisy.

Mini-batch gradient descent updates weights based on a small batch of data, striking a balance between speed and accuracy. Adam, a more advanced optimization algorithm, adapts the learning rate for each parameter, making it efficient and effective for training deep networks.

## 9. Overfitting and Regularization

Overfitting occurs when a model learns the training data too well, including noise and irrelevant patterns, which leads to poor generalization to new, unseen data. To prevent overfitting, regularization techniques are used. Common regularization methods for ANNs include L1 and L2 regularization, which penalize large weights, and dropout, which randomly disables neurons during training. These techniques help improve the network's ability to generalize and avoid overfitting.

## 10. Deep Learning and Multi-Layer Networks

Deep learning refers to the use of deep neural networks, which are ANNs with many hidden layers. The depth of these networks allows them to learn hierarchical features, making them particularly effective in tasks such as image recognition, speech recognition, and natural language processing. Deep learning models, such as Convolutional Neural Networks (CNNs) and Recurrent Neural Networks (RNNs), have become the cornerstone of modern machine learning due to their ability to handle large, complex datasets and extract meaningful patterns.

## 11. Convolutional Neural Networks (CNNs)

CNNs are a specialized type of neural network designed for processing grid-like data, such as images. They use convolutional layers to apply filters (kernels) to input data, extracting low-level features like edges and textures. These features are then passed through pooling layers, which downsample the data to reduce dimensionality. CNNs are highly effective in computer vision tasks, such as image classification, object detection, and segmentation, due to their ability to learn spatial hierarchies of features.

## 12. Recurrent Neural Networks (RNNs)

RNNs are designed to handle sequential data, such as time series or text. Unlike feedforward networks, RNNs have loops in their architecture, allowing them to retain information from previous time steps. This makes them suitable for tasks like language modeling, sentiment analysis, and speech recognition. However, traditional RNNs struggle with long-range dependencies due to the vanishing gradient problem, which is addressed by more advanced models like Long Short-Term Memory (LSTM) networks and Gated Recurrent Units (GRUs).

## 13. Transfer Learning

Transfer learning is a technique where a pre-trained neural network model is used as a starting point for a new task. Instead of training a model from scratch, the weights of an existing model are fine-tuned on a smaller dataset related to the target task. This is particularly useful when the available data for the new task is limited, and it can significantly reduce training time and computational resources. Transfer learning has become a powerful approach, especially in image recognition and natural language processing.

### 14. Applications of Artificial Neural Networks

ANNs are applied in a wide range of domains. In healthcare, they are used for disease diagnosis, medical image analysis, and drug discovery. In finance, ANNs are employed for fraud detection, algorithmic trading, and risk assessment. In natural language processing, ANNs power applications like machine translation, chatbots, and sentiment analysis. In autonomous systems, such as self-driving cars, neural networks are used for decision-making, object detection, and path planning.

### 15. Future Directions in ANN Research

As computational resources continue to grow, the field of artificial neural networks is evolving rapidly. Current research focuses on improving model efficiency, interpretability, and generalization. Techniques like attention mechanisms, neural architecture search, and reinforcement learning are advancing the capabilities of neural networks. Furthermore, there is an increasing emphasis on ethical considerations, ensuring that neural networks are transparent, fair, and used responsibly in applied machine learning tasks. The future of ANNs promises even more breakthroughs in artificial intelligence and machine learning.

## 3.4 FEED FORWARD NEURAL NETWORKS

### 1. Introduction to Feedforward Neural Networks (FNNs)

Feedforward Neural Networks (FNNs) are a type of artificial neural network where the information flows in one direction, from the input layer through the hidden layers to the output layer, without any loops or cycles. This simple structure contrasts with other types of neural networks, like recurrent neural networks (RNNs), where the data can loop back to earlier layers. FNNs are foundational models in applied machine learning, often used for classification and regression tasks, making them one of the most widely studied and used network architectures in the field.

### 2. Structure of a Feedforward Neural Network

A basic feedforward neural network consists of three primary layers:

- **Input Layer:** This layer receives the features of the input data, such as pixel values in an image or feature values in a dataset.
- **Hidden Layers:** One or more hidden layers process the input data using weights, biases, and activation functions. These layers enable the network to learn complex representations of the input data.
- **Output Layer:** The output layer produces the final prediction or classification result based on the learned information. In a classification task, this could be a class label; for regression, it might be a continuous value.

### 3. Neurons and Activation Functions

Each neuron in an FNN is a computational unit that receives inputs from the previous layer, applies weights, and adds a bias term. The result is then passed through an activation function, which introduces non-linearity to the network. Common activation functions include:

- **Sigmoid:** Outputs a value between 0 and 1, often used in binary classification problems.

- **ReLU (Rectified Linear Unit):** Outputs zero for negative inputs and the input itself for positive inputs, making it efficient for training deep networks.
- **Tanh:** Produces outputs in the range between -1 and 1, often used when zero-centered output is desired.
- **Softmax:** Used in multi-class classification tasks, it converts raw output scores into probabilities for each class.

## 4. The Role of Weights and Biases

The weights in an FNN determine the strength and direction of the connection between neurons. Each input to a neuron is multiplied by a weight, which is learned during training to minimize prediction errors. Additionally, each neuron has a bias term that allows the activation function to be shifted, providing flexibility in the model. Weights and biases are adjusted during training to reduce the difference between predicted and actual outputs, which is achieved through optimization techniques like gradient descent.

## 5. Forward Propagation Process

Forward propagation refers to the process of passing input data through the layers of the network to generate an output. In this process, the input is fed into the input layer, and for each hidden layer, the weighted sum of inputs is calculated, passed through an activation function, and forwarded to the next layer. In the output layer, the final result is produced. The forward propagation step is where the network makes its prediction or classification.

## 6. Loss Function

The loss function is used to measure the error between the network's prediction and the actual target values. In supervised learning tasks, the goal is to minimize the loss function. Common loss functions include:

- **Mean Squared Error (MSE):** Typically used in regression problems to calculate the squared difference between predicted and actual values.
- **Cross-Entropy Loss:** Used in classification tasks to measure the difference between the predicted probability distribution and the true class distribution.

## 7. Backpropagation and Error Calculation

Backpropagation is the core algorithm for training FNNs. After forward propagation, the network calculates the error using the loss function. The backpropagation process involves calculating the gradient of the loss with respect to each weight and bias in the network using the chain rule of calculus. These gradients are then used to update the weights and biases in a way that reduces the error, improving the model's performance.

## 8. Gradient Descent Optimization

Once the gradients are calculated during backpropagation, an optimization algorithm like gradient descent is used to update the weights and biases. Gradient descent aims to minimize the loss function by adjusting the weights in the opposite direction of the gradient. There are several variants of gradient descent:

- **Batch Gradient Descent:** Updates weights after processing the entire dataset.
- **Stochastic Gradient Descent (SGD):** Updates weights after processing each individual data point, leading to faster but noisier updates.

- **Mini-Batch Gradient Descent:** A compromise between the two, where weights are updated after processing small batches of data.

## 9. Training Feedforward Neural Networks

Training an FNN involves iterating through the dataset multiple times (epochs), where the weights and biases are updated after each pass through the data. The optimization process continues until the network reaches a point where the error no longer improves or starts to increase, indicating that the model has either converged or is overfitting.

## 10. Overfitting and Regularization Techniques

Overfitting happens when a model learns the training data too well, including noise and irrelevant patterns, which hampers its ability to generalize to new data. Regularization techniques are used to mitigate overfitting:

- **L1 and L2 Regularization:** These techniques add a penalty term to the loss function based on the magnitude of the weights, discouraging large weights.
- **Dropout:** Randomly drops neurons during training to prevent the network from becoming too reliant on any single neuron or set of features.
- **Early Stopping:** Stops training when performance on a validation set starts to degrade, preventing the model from overfitting to the training data.

## 11. Hyperparameter Tuning

Feedforward neural networks involve several hyperparameters that must be tuned for optimal performance:

- **Learning Rate:** Controls the size of the weight updates during training. A learning rate that is too high can cause the model to converge too quickly or miss the optimal solution, while a rate too low can slow down training.
- **Number of Hidden Layers and Neurons:** The depth and width of the network affect its ability to model complex patterns. Too few neurons or layers can lead to underfitting, while too many can lead to overfitting and increased computational cost.
- **Batch Size:** Determines how many data samples are processed before the weights are updated during training.

## 12. Applications of Feedforward Neural Networks

Feedforward neural networks have wide applications in many machine learning tasks. Some of their uses include:

- **Image Classification:** In computer vision, FNNs can be used to classify images into predefined categories.
- **Speech Recognition:** FNNs can recognize speech patterns and convert them into text.
- **Predictive Modeling:** In finance or healthcare, FNNs are used to predict stock prices, patient outcomes, or future trends.
- **Function Approximation:** FNNs are often applied to approximate complex mathematical functions, particularly in engineering and physical sciences.

## 13. Limitations of Feedforward Neural Networks

Despite their simplicity and versatility, feedforward neural networks have several limitations:

- **Lack of Temporal or Sequential Modeling:** FNNs are not well-suited for tasks that involve sequential or time-series data, like language modeling or stock price prediction. Recurrent Neural Networks (RNNs) or Transformers are more appropriate for these tasks.
- **Difficulty in Handling Complex Patterns:** Although FNNs can learn non-linear patterns, very deep networks can suffer from problems like vanishing gradients or require significant computational resources to train effectively.

## 14. Advantages of Feedforward Neural Networks

Feedforward Neural Networks offer several advantages:

- **Simplicity and Interpretability:** They are relatively simple to understand and implement compared to more complex architectures like CNNs or RNNs.
- **Wide Applicability:** FNNs can be applied to a variety of tasks, including regression, classification, and time-series forecasting, making them a versatile tool in machine learning.
- **Scalability:** FNNs can handle large datasets effectively, especially when trained with powerful optimization techniques and hardware like GPUs.

## 15. Future Developments in Feedforward Neural Networks

Although more advanced neural networks like CNNs and RNNs dominate specific domains, FNNs remain essential for many machine learning applications. Research continues to explore methods for improving the efficiency of FNNs, including better training algorithms, more effective regularization techniques, and integration with other types of neural networks. Additionally, hybrid architectures combining feedforward networks with other deep learning models are becoming more common, allowing practitioners to leverage the strengths of multiple approaches for more robust performance in complex tasks.

## UNIT SUMMARY

- This unit provides a comprehensive overview of **neural networks**, a fundamental component of modern artificial intelligence and deep learning. It begins by exploring the **characteristics of neural networks**, highlighting their ability to recognize complex patterns, learn from data, and generalize across different tasks. These networks mimic the structure and functionality of the human brain, making them powerful tools for solving problems in fields such as image recognition, natural language processing, and financial forecasting.
- The unit then traces the **historical development of neural network principles**, detailing key milestones from early perceptron models to the evolution of deep learning. The discussion of **Artificial Neural Networks (ANNs)** introduces their structure, including neurons, activation functions, and learning algorithms, which enable them to adapt and improve performance over time. Finally, the unit covers **Feedforward Neural Networks (FNNs)**, one of the simplest and most widely used architectures, where information flows in a single direction without feedback loops. These foundational concepts set the stage for understanding more advanced neural network architectures and their applications in real-world scenarios.

## EXERCISE

### 2-Mark Questions

1. Define a neural network.
2. List any two characteristics of neural networks.
3. State the significance of activation functions in neural networks.
4. What is a perceptron in the context of neural networks?
5. Differentiate between biological and artificial neural networks.
6. Mention two applications of feedforward neural networks.
7. When were the first neural network models developed?
8. Name two types of activation functions used in artificial neural networks.
9. Identify the main components of an artificial neural network.
10. What is the primary limitation of early perceptron models?

### 16 -Mark Questions

1. Explain the key characteristics of neural networks and their importance in artificial intelligence.
2. Discuss the historical evolution of neural networks, highlighting key milestones in their development.
3. Describe the structure and working of an artificial neural network with a neat diagram.
4. Compare and contrast feedforward neural networks and recurrent neural networks in terms of structure and applications.
5. Analyze the role of activation functions in neural networks and justify their necessity.
6. Illustrate the working of a perceptron model and explain its significance in neural networks.
7. Evaluate the strengths and limitations of feedforward neural networks in machine learning applications.
8. Apply the concept of neural networks to a real-world problem, explaining how they can be used for predictive analysis.
9. Design a simple artificial neural network architecture for an image classification task and justify your design choices.
10. Critically assess the impact of neural networks on modern artificial intelligence and future technological advancements.

❖❖❖

Unit **4**

# Data Clustering & Decision Tree Learning

## Rationale

Clustering and decision tree learning are fundamental techniques in machine learning that help in pattern recognition, classification, and predictive modeling. This unit introduces essential clustering methods and decision tree algorithms, which are widely used in applications such as market segmentation, anomaly detection, and decision-making systems.

The unit begins with an overview of clustering, followed by a discussion of different types of clustering methods, including K-Means, Fuzzy K-Means, Expectation-Maximization (EM) Algorithm, and Gaussian Mixtures Clustering. These techniques help in identifying hidden patterns within datasets without predefined labels, making them useful for unsupervised learning tasks. Additionally, Principal Component Analysis (PCA) is introduced as a dimensionality reduction technique, which enhances model efficiency by eliminating redundant features. Rough sets-based methods are also explored as an alternative approach for handling uncertainty in data classification.

The second part of the unit focuses on decision tree learning, a powerful classification technique used for making structured, rule-based predictions. An example of a classification decision tree is discussed to illustrate how these models work. The concept of pruning is covered to optimize decision trees by reducing overfitting. Finally, the unit introduces fuzzy decision trees, which enhance traditional decision trees by incorporating fuzzy logic, allowing for better handling of uncertainty and imprecise data. By understanding these clustering and decision tree techniques, learners will gain the ability to apply unsupervised and supervised learning methods to solve complex machine learning problems effectively.

## 4.1 OVERVIEW OF CLUSTERING

Clustering is an unsupervised learning technique used to group similar data points. It helps in data segmentation, pattern recognition, and anomaly detection. Unlike classification, clustering does not require labeled data. Clustering is widely used in various domains, including:

- **Marketing:** Customer segmentation for targeted advertising.
- **Healthcare:** Disease classification and medical imaging.
- **Cybersecurity:** Anomaly detection in network security.

- **Finance:** Credit risk analysis and fraud detection.
- **Image Processing:** Object recognition and image compression.

## 4.2 TYPES OF CLUSTERING METHODS

- **Partition-based Clustering:** Divides data into k clusters (e.g., K-Means).
- **Density-based Clustering:** Groups data based on high-density regions (e.g., DBSCAN).
- **Hierarchical Clustering:** Forms a tree-like structure (e.g., Agglomerative).
- **Model-based Clustering:** Uses probabilistic models (e.g., Gaussian Mixtures).
- **Grid-based Clustering:** Organizes data into grids before clustering (e.g., STING).

## 4.3 K-MEANS CLUSTERING

K-Means clustering is a widely used unsupervised machine learning algorithm that groups data into K distinct clusters based on similarity. It is commonly applied in areas such as customer segmentation, anomaly detection, image compression, and recommendation systems.This algorithm minimizes intra-cluster variance by assigning data points to the nearest cluster centroid and updating centroids iteratively.

### 4.3.1 Working Principle of K-Means Algorithm

The K-Means algorithm follows an iterative approach with the following steps:

**Step 1:** Choose K (Number of Clusters):

- The number of clusters (K) must be predefined.
- The choice of K affects clustering performance.

**Step 2:** Initialize Centroids:

- Randomly select K data points as the initial cluster centers.
- Centroids act as representative points for each cluster.

**Step 3:** Assignment Step:

- Compute the Euclidean distance between each data point and all centroids.
- Assign each data point to the nearest centroid.

**Step 4 :** Update Step:

- Compute the new centroids by taking the mean of all points in each cluster.

**Step 5:** Repeat Until Convergence:

- The algorithm repeats steps 3 and 4 until the centroids no longer change significantly.

## 4.4 FUZZY K-MEANS CLUSTERING

In data clustering, defining the type of data partitioning is essential. There are two primary types: hard and soft partitions. The K-means algorithm is an example of hard partitioning, where each data point belongs exclusively to one cluster. However, in many real-world scenarios, strict cluster separation may not be feasible. Soft partitioning addresses this issue by allowing data points to belong to multiple clusters with varying degrees of membership. This approach extends hard partitioning by accommodating cases where objects cannot be distinctly assigned to a single category.

In K-means clustering, each data point is assigned to a single, non-overlapping cluster. Conversely, in Fuzzy K-Means Clustering, data points can belong to multiple clusters with membership values between 0 and 1. This method acknowledges that clusters often overlap, making it difficult to establish precise boundaries. As a result, some data points are better represented by partial memberships across multiple clusters. A key constraint in this approach is that the sum of membership values for a given data point across all clusters must equal 1.

Fuzzy K-Means Clustering, also known as Fuzzy C-Means (FCM), is an extension of the traditional K-Means algorithm that allows data points to belong to multiple clusters with varying degrees of membership. Unlike K-Means, which assigns each point to a single cluster, FCM introduces the concept of soft clustering, where each point has a membership value between 0 and 1 for different clusters. This approach is particularly useful when dealing with overlapping data distributions, where strict boundaries between clusters are difficult to define.

1. **Membership Degree:** Each data point is assigned a membership value for each cluster, indicating the likelihood of the point belonging to that cluster. The membership values range between 0 and 1, and the sum of all memberships for a single data point across all clusters must equal 1.
2. **Cluster Centers:** Similar to K-Means, FCM computes cluster centroids, but their positions are influenced by the membership degrees of data points. A data point contributes more to a centroid's computation if it has a higher membership value for that cluster.
3. **Fuzziness Parameter (m):** The algorithm introduces a fuzzification parameter m (typically greater than 1), which controls the level of cluster overlap.Higher values of m result in more overlapping clusters, while lower values make the clusters more distinct, approaching the behavior of hard clustering.

## Advantages of Fuzzy K-Means

- **Handles Uncertain Data:** Ideal for datasets where clear-cut boundaries do not exist.
- **More Flexible than K-Means:** Allows data points to belong to multiple clusters instead of forcing a hard assignment.
- **Better Representation of Real-World Data:** Many practical applications involve overlapping categories, making soft clustering more appropriate.

## Limitations of Fuzzy K-Means

- **Computational Complexity:** Higher than K-Means due to repeated calculations of membership values.
- **Choice of Fuzziness Parameter:** The performance depends on selecting an appropriate m value, which may require tuning.
- **Sensitive to Initial Conditions:** Similar to K-Means, different initializations may lead to different results.

## Applications of Fuzzy K-Means

- **Image Segmentation:** Used in medical imaging and computer vision to classify pixels into different regions.

- **Pattern Recognition:** Useful in speech recognition and handwriting analysis.
- **Customer Segmentation:** Helps categorize customers into overlapping segments based on buying behavior.
- **Bioinformatics:** Used for gene expression data analysis and protein classification.

Fuzzy K-Means Clustering provides a more flexible and realistic approach to clustering compared to traditional K-Means. By allowing partial membership in multiple clusters, it effectively handles overlapping datasets and uncertainty in data classification. However, it requires careful tuning of parameters and has a higher computational cost. Despite these challenges, it is widely used in various fields, including image processing, machine learning, and data science.

Additionally, if a data point is nearly equidistant from all cluster centers, it may be considered noise. In such cases, its membership values should be relatively low for all clusters. However, the requirement that the total membership across clusters sums to 1 must still be upheld.

## 4.5 EXPECTATION-MAXIMIZATION (EM) ALGORITHM

The Expectation-Maximization (EM) algorithm is a powerful iterative approach used in data clustering, particularly for probabilistic models like Gaussian Mixture Models (GMM). Unlike traditional clustering techniques such as K-Means, which assign data points to a single cluster, EM estimates the probability that a point belongs to each cluster. This makes it especially useful for handling datasets with overlapping clusters or missing data.

1. **Latent Variables:** EM assumes that the observed data is generated by an underlying probabilistic process involving hidden (latent) variables. These latent variables determine the cluster assignments but are not directly observed.
2. **Probabilistic Clustering:** Instead of assigning a hard label to each data point, EM computes the probability of a point belonging to each cluster. This allows soft clustering, where data points have fractional memberships in multiple clusters.
3. **Likelihood Function:** The algorithm aims to maximize the likelihood of the observed data given the assumed probability distributions of clusters.
4. **Expectation (E) Step:** Estimates the probability (responsibility) of each data point belonging to each cluster based on current parameters.
5. **Maximization (M) Step:** Updates the cluster parameters (mean, variance, and mixing coefficients) to maximize the likelihood of the observed data.

### Advantages of EM Algorithm

- **Soft Clustering:** Unlike K-Means, EM provides probabilistic cluster assignments, making it more suitable for overlapping clusters.
- **Handles Missing Data:** EM can infer missing values using probability distributions.
- **Works with Arbitrary Cluster Shapes:** Since EM uses Gaussian distributions, it can model elliptical and non-spherical clusters better than K-Means.

### Limitations of EM Algorithm

- **Computational Complexity:** More computationally expensive than K-Means, especially for high-dimensional data.

- **Sensitive to Initialization:** Poor initial values can lead to local optima.
- **Requires the Number of Clusters:** Similar to K-Means, the number of clusters \( K \) must be specified beforehand.

### Applications of EM Algorithm in Clustering

1. **Image Segmentation:** Used for grouping pixels into different categories based on color and texture.
2. **Speech Recognition:** Helps in identifying phonemes in spoken language.
3. **Customer Segmentation:** Groups customers based on behavior patterns.
4. **Anomaly Detection:** Identifies unusual patterns in data, such as fraud detection in finance.
5. **Medical Diagnosis:** Assists in clustering diseases based on patient symptoms.

The Expectation-Maximization (EM) algorithm is a robust approach to probabilistic clustering, offering flexibility in modelling data distributions. By iteratively estimating cluster probabilities and refining model parameters, it effectively captures complex structures in datasets. Despite its computational challenges, EM remains widely used in fields such as machine learning, image processing, and natural language processing.

## 4.6 GAUSSIAN MIXTURES CLUSTERING

Clustering is a fundamental operation in data analysis and machine learning, and it is a question of assembling similar points by exploiting some inherent structure. Typical clustering algorithms such as k-means, for instance, make the assumption of spherical clusters of equal size. However, data tends to come in patterns of subtler structure, patterns which are more difficult to characterize and which partitioning cannot accurately replicate.

Gaussian Mixture Models (GMM) offer a probabilistic method of clustering, in which points are supposed to be drawn from several Gaussian distributions with unknown parameters. By representing data as a mixture of several Gaussian components, GMM offers soft, flexible clustering, which is especially appropriate for data with overlapping clusters or clusters of varying shapes and densities.

### Concept of Gaussian Mixtures

Gaussian Mixture Model is a method of representing a data set in terms of a mixture of multiple Gaussian distributions. In contrast to assigning each data point to a unique cluster, GMM assigns probabilities, so each data point can belong to multiple clusters with varying levels of confidence. This probabilistic nature makes GMM a very efficient alternative to hard clustering algorithms like k-means. Every Gaussian component of the mixture is a potential cluster, each with its parameters, e.g., a central mean, a spread to cover variance, and a weight to cover its contribution to the total data distribution. The parameters decide the shape and direction of every cluster in the feature space.

### Advantages of GMM-Based Clustering

1. **Soft Clustering:** In contrast to k-means, which assigns a point to a single cluster, GMM gives a probability distribution over all the clusters, so more nuanced groupings can be achieved.

2. **Irregular Cluster Shapes:** Since GMM supports ellipsoidal clusters rather than spherical clusters, it also includes cases where clusters are irregularly shaped.
3. **Outlier Robustness:** Robustness to outliers is achieved through probabilistic clustering, which accommodates data uncertainty, thus GMM is more resistant to outliers and noise than hard clustering methods.
4. **More Realistic Modelling of Real-World Data:** The majority of natural data and datasets are Gaussian-distributed, and hence GMM is a more realistic model in fields like finance, biology, and speech recognition.

### Applications of GMM in Clustering

GMM is used in many fields because it can efficiently model complex distributions. Some of its prominent applications are:

- **Image Segmentation:** GMM allows for the identification of different regions of an image through probabilistic modeling of pixel intensity distributions.
- **Speech Recognition:** In acoustic modeling, GMM is used to model phonemes in speech signals to improve speech-to-text translations.
- **Anomaly Detection:** Identifying typical data distributions through learning, GMM is capable of detecting outliers, and therefore is used in fraud detection and network security.
- **Financial Data Analysis:** For identifying financial trend clustering and market segmentation in stock market analysis and risk estimation, GMM is useful.

GMM is particularly beneficial when data clusters are of uneven densities or heavily overlapping clusters. Although k-means is more efficient and faster in computation for big data, GMM is more adaptable at the cost of increased computational complexity.

### Disadvantages of GMM in Clustering

1. **Computational Complexity:** Estimation of parameters in GMM relies upon computationally cumbersome iterative algorithms, particularly for data that is heavy in size.
2. **Selecting the Number of Components:** You need to choose the number of best-fitting components and in most instances, this entails model selection techniques such as the Bayesian Information Criterion (BIC) or the Akaike Information Criterion (AIC).
3. **Convergence to Local Optima:** GMM is based on iterative optimization, which at times leads to convergence to local optima based on initialization.

Gaussian Mixture Models provide a robust model for clustering data when traditional approaches are not effective due to strong assumptions. With probabilistic concepts, GMM enables soft clustering, intricate shapes of clusters, and more interpretable data patterns. Its applications are diverse across domains, indicative of its capacity to address real-world problem-solving. Despite its computational demands, GMM is a valuable tool in the clustering paradigm, offering deeper insights into data distributions.

## 4.7 PRINCIPAL COMPONENTS ANALYSIS (PCA)

Principal Component Analysis (PCA) is a strong dimensionality reduction technique that projects high-dimensional data into lower-dimensional space without losing significant patterns. PCA eliminates noise and redundancy, which enhances clustering performance and enables the easier identification of significant group structures.

PCA is a statistical method that projects a high-dimensional data set whose variables are highly intercorrelated onto a lower-dimensional data set of uncorrelated variables, or principal components. The principal components capture most of the data variability and eliminate less informative dimensions. Each principal component is a linear combination of the original attributes, ordered by the variance that it captures. The first component captures the greatest variance, the second the second greatest variance, and so forth. By keeping only the essential components, PCA compresses the data without compromising its underlying structure.

## PCA Role in Clustering

PCA is never used as a clustering algorithm but is an integral tool towards enhanced clustering performance in the sense that

1. **Dimensionality Reduction:** High-dimensional data tends to be noisy because of redundant features. PCA removes redundant dimensions, and clustering performs better.
2. **Improving Cluster Separation:** By rotating data into a new space, PCA improves the separation between clusters, particularly when correlations between underlying features hide inherent groupings.
3. **Reducing Computational Cost:** The majority of clustering algorithms, such as k-means and Gaussian Mixture Models (GMM), are computationally costly in high dimensions. PCA speeds up computation because PCA reduces the dimensionality of the features.
4. **Reduction of Overfitting:** In high-dimensional data, cluster models can overfit because they have too many features. PCA prevents this from happening by projecting only the significant data patterns.

## Applications of PCA in Clustering

PCA is found in many applications to improve clustering performance. Some of its significant applications are:

1. **Image Compression & Segmentation:** PCA compresses images by reducing dimensions without sacrificing important patterns, thus aiding image segmentation and clustering.
2. **Genomics & Bioinformatics:** For gene and genetic data, where the number of variables is in the thousands, PCA enables the clustering of similar genetic profiles to differentiate diseases.
3. **Market Segmentation:** Companies use PCA to simplify complex customer purchasing behavior information to classify customers into purchasing behavior segments.
4. **Cybersecurity Anomaly Detection:** PCA helps in clustering network traffic patterns such that anomalies that may represent security attacks can be detected.

PCA is effective when raw data contains features that are highly correlated and have latent natural clusters. It can reveal patterns that were not visible in the original space by compressing the data.While PCA enhances clustering in most cases, some problems have to be considered:

1. **Loss of Interpretability:** The transformed major components may not necessarily have a natural, straightforward interpretation in the original feature space.
2. **Reduction Based on Variance:** PCA only cares about retaining variance, which may not be the most suitable features to group.
3. **Sensitive to Scaling:** Results of PCA are influenced by features of varying scales, and therefore appropriate data preprocessing is required before applying PCA.

Principal Component Analysis is a precious method of boosting clustering by reducing high-dimensional data without losing important patterns. By providing greater computational efficiency, noise reduction, and better cluster separation, PCA facilitates more effective clustering in most instances. Except for some limitations, its integration with clustering algorithms remains an essential technique in machine learning and data science.

## 4.8 ROUGH SETS-BASED METHODS

Data clustering and data analysis are key machine learning and knowledge discovery techniques. Yet, data in real-world applications tends to be incomplete, imprecise, or uncertain, reducing the effectiveness of conventional methods. Rough Set Theory (RST) offers a mathematical approach to deal with uncertainty so that efficient data classification, clustering, and decision-making can be achieved without any need for additional probability or membership functions. Proposed by Zdzisław Pawlak in the early 1980s, rough sets find special application in handling imprecise or vague information. Unlike conventional set theory approaches that depend on well-defined boundaries, rough sets permit approximate reasoning, which is useful in medical diagnosis, financial prediction, and pattern recognition, among others.

### Basic Concepts of Rough Set Theory

Rough Set Theory is founded on the concept that real data tends to be imprecise and does not always provide clear classifications. It classifies objects in relation to their attributes and employs approximation regions to indicate uncertainty. The main concepts are:

1. **Information System and Decision Table:** A data set in rough set theory is depicted as an information system with objects (rows) and attributes (columns). The data set can also be organized as a decision table, in which attributes are split into:
   - Condition attributes: Characteristics utilized to represent objects.
   - Decision attributes: Class labels or categories for objects.
2. **Indiscernibility Relation:** In conventional set theory, objects are distinguished into different classes. In rough sets, objects with the same values for some attributes are said to be indiscernible. Such objects cannot be clearly grouped into different categories, resulting in the necessity for approximate reasoning.
3. **Approximation Regions:** Three regions are identified by rough sets to deal with uncertainty:
   - **Lower Approximation:** The collection of objects that certainly fall into a category according to information at hand.

- **Upper Approximation:** The collection of objects that may fall into a category, i.e., they possess features of several categories.
- **Boundary Region:** The set difference of upper and lower approximations, which is a measure of uncertainty in classification.

4. **Reducts and Core Attributes:** Not all features are equally involved in decision-making. Reducts are minimal sets of features that maintain classification power, lowering computational complexity. Core features are the most important features that cannot be eliminated without sacrificing vital information.

Clustering puts similar objects together by feature. Classical methods of clustering like k-means and hierarchical clustering tend to suffer from incomplete or imprecise data. Rough sets assist with:

1. **Uncertainty Handling:** Contrary to crisp clustering, the rough set-based clustering permits the objects to reside in boundary areas, recognizing uncertainty.
2. **Feature Reduction:** Rough sets determine the best features, avoiding high dimensionality and enhancing clustering performance.
3. **Enhancing Interpretability:** By establishing lower and upper approximations, rough sets offer a better interpretation of imprecise clusters.

## Hybrid Rough Set Clustering Methods

- **Rough k-Means Clustering:** Improves k-means by integrating rough approximations, enabling soft clustering of fuzzy objects.
- **Fuzzy-Rough Clustering:** Integrates rough sets with fuzzy logic, providing degrees of membership with boundary regions.
- **Rough Hierarchical Clustering:** Employs rough approximations to enhance hierarchical clustering outputs.

## Applications of Rough Sets-Based Methods

Rough sets have been applied successfully in a wide range of applications, including:

1. **Medical Diagnosis:** Facilitates disease identification from incomplete patient information.
2. **Intrusion Detection Systems:** Increases security by detecting uncertain patterns in network traffic.
3. **Market Segmentation:** Segments customers on the basis of imprecise behavioral patterns.
4. **Financial Risk Analysis:** Evaluates uncertain financial trends in order to forecast risks.

## Challenges and Considerations

Although rough set-based techniques have several benefits, they have challenges as well:

1. **Computational Cost:** Large datasets need efficient algorithms in order to calculate approximations.
2. **Dependency on Attribute Quality:** Low-quality attributes can affect the effectiveness of clustering.

3. **Interpretability of Results:** Although rough sets enhance comprehension, the outcomes can still need to be interpreted by an expert.

Rough set-based approaches offer a powerful means of coping with uncertainty in data analysis and clustering. Using lower and upper approximations, rough sets represent a flexible and interpretable mechanism for dealing with imprecise data. Through their combination with other machine learning methods, like fuzzy logic and deep learning, their applications extend to many different fields.

## 4.9 CLASSIFICATION DECISION TREE

Decision trees are among the most popular classification and decision-making methods in machine learning. They are a methodical approach to making predictions by partitioning a dataset into subsets according to feature values.

The tree structure renders decision-making understandable, efficient, and simple to apply, and therefore it is well-liked in medical diagnosis, finance, and customer segmentation. A classification decision tree is a supervised learning method that maps an input to a node label based on its features. It operates by recursively partitioning the set of data into subsets, resulting in a hierarchy leading to a conclusion.

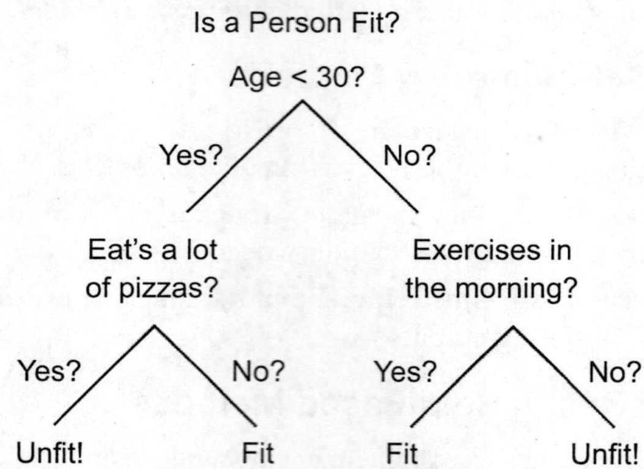


### Decision Tree Concept

A classification decision tree has the following principal components:

1. **Root Node:** The root of the tree, that is, the entire dataset. It holds the most informative feature that assists in dividing the data into various classes.
2. **Internal Nodes:** They are decision points in which the dataset is partitioned further considering a feature's value.
3. **Branches:** Each of these represents an outcome of a decision taken at an internal node.
4. **Leaf Nodes:** They are the end nodes where decisions about classification are taken. One leaf node symbolizes a class label given to instances after traveling down that path.

**Building a classification decision tree entails the following steps:**

**Step 1:** Selecting the Best Attribute: At every node, the algorithm chooses the most appropriate attribute to divide the data. This is done based on criteria like:

- **Gini Impurity:** Indicates how frequently a randomly selected element would be misclassified.
- **Entropy (Information Gain):** A disorder measure, with increased information gain reflecting a good split.

**Step 2:** Splitting the Dataset: After the optimal attribute is selected, the dataset is split into subsets according to its values. This is done recursively until stopping criteria are reached.

**Step 3:** Stopping Criteria: The tree is halted when:

- All instances in a node are of the same class.
- There are no more attributes to split.
- The tree goes to a predetermined depth limit.

**Step 4:** Class Label Assignment: Once the tree is at a leaf node, a final classification decision is taken, classifying the data point with a label.

**Example of a Classification Decision Tree:**

- Scenario: Loan Approval Prediction: A bank wishes to automate loan approval on the basis of customer features like income level, credit score, and existing debts. The class labels are:
  - ♦ Approved (Loan granted)
  - ♦ Denied (Loan not granted)

| Customer | Income Level | Credit Score | Existing Debts | Loan Approved? | Customer |
|---|---|---|---|---|---|
| A | High | Good | No | Approved | A |
| B | Medium | Good | No | Approved | B |
| C | Medium | Poor | Yes | Denied | C |
| D | Low | Good | No | Approved | D |
| E | Low | Poor | Yes | Denied | E |

**Decision Tree Construction:**

1. **Selecting the First Attribute:** The best attribute to split on might be Credit Score, as it significantly impacts loan approval.
2. **Splitting Data:**
   - ♦ If Credit Score = Good, further check Income Level.
   - ♦ If Credit Score = Poor, classify as Denied.
3. **Further Splitting on Income Level:**
   - ♦ If Income = High or Medium, classify as Approved.
   - ♦ If Income = Low, further check Existing Debts.
4. **Final Decision:**
   - ♦ If Existing Debts = No, classify as Approved.
   - ♦ If Existing Debts = Yes, classify as Denied.

**Resulting Decision Tree**

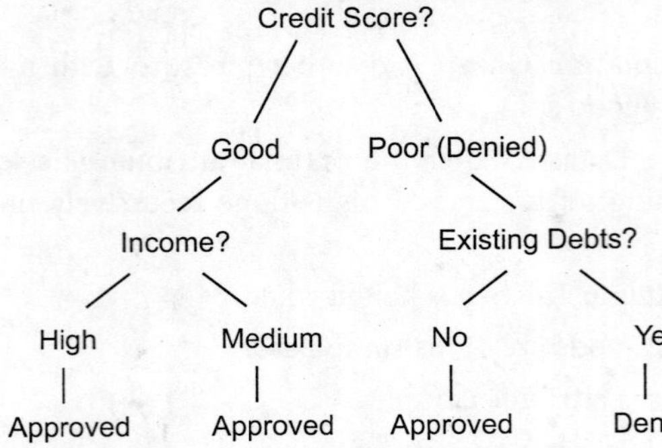


For a new customer, the decision tree proceeds in a direction determined by the given attributes, finally predicting loan approval or denial.

### Advantages of Decision Trees

1. **Easy to Interpret:** The hierarchical structure makes it easier for humans to make decisions.
2. **Handles Non-Linear Relationships:** Captures complex patterns without requiring mathematical transformations.
3. **Feature Selection Built-in:** Automatically identifies important attributes.
4. **Works on Mixed Data Types:** Can handle both numerical and categorical data.

### Challenges and Limitations:

- **Overfitting:** Deep trees may become too specific to training data, reducing generalization.
- **Bias Towards Dominant Classes:** If the dataset is imbalanced, the tree can be biased towards majority classes.
- **Sensitivity to Noisy Data:** The tree structures can differ substantially due to small variations in data.

Classification decision trees offer a simple and powerful way of making predictions from structured decisions. Their capacity to process complex data, along with their interpretability, makes them an important tool in machine learning and practical applications. Decision trees can be improved for better performance using ensemble methods such as Random Forests or pruning to minimize overfitting.

## 4.9.1 Id3, C4.5, And Cart Decision Trees

Decision tree learning algorithms are popularly applied in machine learning to classification and regression problems. They provide an intuitive, rule-based style of decision-making by recursively partitioning datasets according to attribute values. Some of the most popular decision tree algorithms include ID3 (Iterative Dichotomiser 3), C4.5 (successor of ID3), and CART (Classification and Regression Trees). Each algorithm has a systematic methodology to build decision trees but varies according to how they treat data, splitting rules, and pruning strategies.

This chapter delves into the fundamentals, techniques, and variances among these decision tree algorithms with the purpose of informing their usage and application on various tasks.

## 1. ID3 (Iterative Dichotomiser 3) Decision Tree

ID3 was created by Ross Quinlan in 1986 and is one of the oldest decision tree algorithms. It is mainly used for categorical data and has information gain as its splitting criterion.

### *How ID3 Works*

1. **Choose the Root Attribute:** The algorithm begins with the whole dataset and chooses the attribute that gives the greatest information gain (i.e., the most informative attribute).
2. **Recursive Splitting:** The dataset is divided on the basis of the chosen attribute's values, forming branches.
3. **Stopping Condition:** The recursion ends when all elements in a subset have the same class or there are no remaining attributes for splitting.

### *Splitting Criterion: Information Gain*

ID3 employs Entropy to quantify impurity of a dataset and Information Gain to calculate the optimal attribute for splitting. Attributes with greater information gain are utilized first as they minimize uncertainty in classification.

### *Limitations of ID3*

Is applicable only for categorical attributes (does not support numerical values). Prone to overfitting in noisy data. Is not able to deal with missing values efficiently.

## 2. C4.5 Decision Tree

C4.5, also created by Ross Quinlan, is a refinement of ID3. It improves upon ID3's shortcomings by supporting numerical attributes, dealing with missing values, and adding pruning to avoid overfitting.

### *How C4.5 Works*

1. **Supports Both Categorical and Numerical Data:** In contrast to ID3, C4.5 supports continuous attributes by generating threshold-based splits.
2. **Utilizes Gain Ratio for Splitting:** Rather than using Information Gain alone, C4.5 adds Gain Ratio, which corrects for bias in favor of attributes with numerous values.
3. **Handles Missing Values:** If a value of an attribute is missing, C4.5 approximates it based on other attribute values using probabilities.
4. **Performs Pruning to Avoid Overfitting:** Once the tree is built, C4.5 performs post-pruning by eliminating branches that do not have a significant impact on classification.

### *Splitting Criterion: Gain Ratio*

C4.5 employs Gain Ratio, which is an improvement over Information Gain in that it normalizes it with the split information (attribute value distribution measure). This is to avoid attributes with a high number of distinct values from dominating the decision-making process.

### Advantages of C4.5

Works with both categorical and numerical attributes. Reduces overfitting with pruning. Handles missing values effectively. More robust compared to ID3.

### Limitations of C4.5

Computationally more expensive than ID3.Gain Ratio can sometimes overcompensate, ignoring useful attributes.

## 3. CART (Classification and Regression Trees)

CART, designed by Breiman et al., is another widely used decision tree algorithm. In contrast to ID3 and C4.5, CART is intended for both classification and regression problems. CART builds binary trees based on the Gini Index as its splitting function.

### How CART Works

1. **Binary Splitting Only:** As opposed to C4.5, which supports multi-way splits, CART always splits nodes into two.
2. **Uses Gini Impurity for Splitting:** CART employs the Gini Index, which is a measure of how frequently a randomly selected element would be misclassified, instead of Entropy or Gain Ratio.
3. **Handles Both Classification and Regression:** CART is applicable both to classification (decision trees) and regression (predicting continuous values).
4. **Pruning to Prevent Overfitting:** Applies cost-complexity pruning, which deletes splits that do not enhance accuracy.

### Splitting Criterion: Gini Index

The Gini Index quantifies data purity, favoring attributes with the purest subsets. Lower values on the Gini Index represent better splits.

### Advantages of CART

Accommodates numerical and categorical data. Operates on both classification and regression. Binary splits simplify computation.

### Limitations of CART

Does not compute probabilities for predictions. More prone to overfitting compared to C4.5 if pruning is not applied.

## Applications of Decision Tree Algorithms

1. **ID3:** Simple classification problems with categorical attributes, e.g., spam detection.
2. **C4.5:** Advanced classification problems with mixed data types, i.e., medical diagnosis and customer segmentation.
3. **CART:** Both classification and regression problems, e.g., credit risk assessment and house price forecasting.

ID3, C4.5, and CART are core decision tree algorithms that have influenced contemporary machine learning. ID3 set the foundation, while C4.5 built on it by adding handling of numerical data as well as pruning. CART brought a general-purpose approach that can be applied to classification and regression problems. All the algorithms have their merits and are best used for particular types of problems and hence are necessary utilities in data science and artificial intelligence.

## 4.10 PRUNING

Decision trees are strong machine learning algorithms applied in classification and regression problems. Yet, they usually experience overfitting such that the tree gets excessively complicated by taking noise or extraneous patterns within the training dataset.

Pruning is a method utilized to reduce the complexity of decision trees by dropping less important branches, enhancing the generalization capacity, and resulting in better performance on unseen datasets.

This chapter discusses the notion of pruning, various pruning strategies, and their use in decision tree algorithms like C4.5 and CART.Pruning refers to the process of shrinking the size of a decision tree by eliminating nodes and branches that have minimal impact on predictive accuracy. Pruning aids in preventing overfitting and enhances the capacity of the tree to generalize well to new data.

### Why Pruning is Required?

1. **Avoids Overfitting:** Trees that are too deep pick up noise instead of general trends.
2. **Simplifies Complexity:** A pruned tree is simpler to understand and involves fewer calculations.
3. **Better Generalization:** A pruned tree can handle new data better, decreasing error rates.
4. **Improves Model Efficiency:** Eliminating useless nodes accelerates predictions and training.

### Types of Pruning

Pruning is generally classified into two types:

### *1. Pre-Pruning (Early Stopping)*

Pre-pruning, also known as early stopping, prevents the tree from growing too deep during the construction phase. This is done by setting constraints such as:

- **Maximum Tree Depth:** Limits the depth of the tree.
- **Minimum Samples per Leaf Node:** Ensures each leaf node has a sufficient number of instances.
- **Information Gain Threshold:** Stops further splits if the gain in information is too small.

#### *Advantages of Pre-Pruning*

Reduces training time by stopping unnecessary splits. Prevents overfitting early. Ensures a more generalizable model.

#### *Disadvantages of Pre-Pruning*

Tends to overfit the data in the worst region. Difficulty in having a clear view of optimal pruning criteria.

### 2. Post-Pruning (Pruning After Tree Construction)

Post-pruning occurs by growing the complete tree and subsequently eliminating subtrees that contribute minimally towards accuracy. Post-pruning is accomplished with the help of statistical methods that compare the subtree's contribution to each to the measure of prediction performance.

#### Techniques for Post-Pruning

A. **Reduced Error Pruning (REP):** Most basic type of pruning. Eliminates nodes if they don't increase accuracy on a validation set. Compares pre- and post-pruning errors; if accuracy increases or stays the same, the node is eliminated.

B. **Cost-Complexity Pruning (CCP) (Implemented in CART):** Also referred to as Weakest Link Pruning. Trades off between model accuracy and tree complexity through the imposition of a complexity penalty. Tunes the strength of pruning using a hyperparameter ($\alpha$).

C. **Minimum Error Pruning:** Checks the error rate of the tree with cross-validation. Prunes branches that raise the general error rate.

D. **Pessimistic Pruning (Used in C4.5):** Proposed by Ross Quinlan in C4.5 to prevent overfitting. Predicts the actual error of a subtree and prunes if it grows.

#### Advantages of Post-Pruning

Better than pre-pruning since it tests the whole tree. Preserves key patterns while eliminating irrelevant details. Enhances the accuracy on new data.

#### Disadvantages of Post-Pruning

Computationally costly, since it needs validation sets or cross-validation. Needs extra decision criteria for pruning efficiency.

## Applications of Pruning

Pruning is commonly applied in a wide range of fields to improve decision-making processes:

- **Medical Diagnosis:** Streamlines trees employed to make disease prediction from symptoms easier.
- **Fraud Detection:** Limits overfitting for financial fraud classification.
- **Customer Segmentation:** Facilitates identifying major customer groups without unwanted complexity.
- **Spam Filtering:** Enhances correctness by avoiding overfitting for rare patterns.

## Challenges and Considerations in Pruning

Selecting the appropriate pruning technique: Various datasets need varying pruning techniques. Cost of computation: Post-pruning is computationally expensive. Avoiding underfitting and overfitting: Pre-pruning has the potential to cause underfitting if overdone.

Pruning is a critical decision tree learning technique that helps maintain models interpretable, efficient, and generalizable. Pre-pruning avoids over-growing the tree during training, while post-pruning reduces an already fully grown tree by eliminating redundant complexity. Proper knowledge and implementation of the appropriate pruning technique increase the dependability and accuracy of decision trees across applications.

## 4.11 FUZZY DECISION TREES

Decision trees are widely used for classification and regression tasks due to their simplicity, interpretability, and effectiveness. However, traditional decision trees like ID3, C4.5, and CART struggle with handling uncertainty, vagueness, and imprecise data. To address these limitations, Fuzzy Decision Trees (FDTs) integrate fuzzy logic with traditional decision tree structures, allowing for gradual classification rather than strict, binary decisions. Fuzzy decision trees are particularly useful in real-world applications where data is ambiguous, such as medical diagnosis, customer preference analysis, and financial risk assessment.

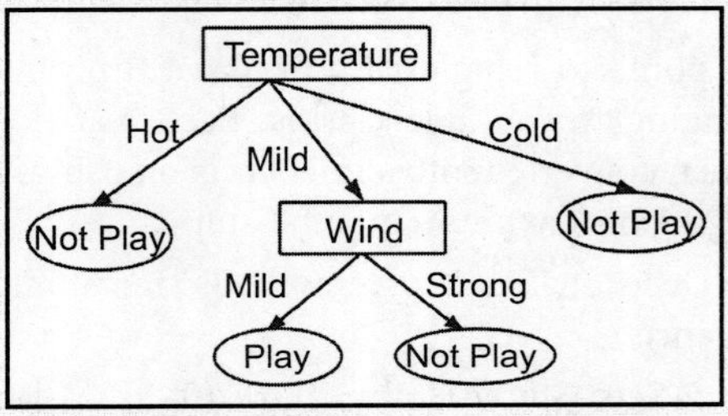


***Fig. 4.1*** *Fuzzy Decision Tree Example*

A Fuzzy Decision Tree (FDT) is an extension of a conventional decision tree that incorporates fuzzy logic principles. Instead of making hard splits (e.g., "if age > 40, then yes; otherwise, no"), an FDT assigns membership degrees to different classes based on fuzzy sets.For example, instead of categorizing "age" as just young or old, an FDT may classify it as "young (0.8), middle-aged (0.5), and old (0.2)", allowing for smoother transitions between classes.

### Key Features of FDTs

- **Handles Uncertainty:** Works well with noisy or imprecise data.
- **Uses Fuzzy Membership Functions:** Assigns degrees of belonging to different categories.
- **Soft Decision Boundaries:** Overcomes the rigid splitting in traditional decision trees.
- **Better Generalization:** Reduces overfitting by incorporating uncertainty into the decision-making process.

### How Fuzzy Decision Trees Work

#### *1. Fuzzification (Defining Fuzzy Sets)*

In FDTs, continuous attributes (e.g., temperature, speed, income) are transformed into fuzzy sets using membership functions. This process is called fuzzification.For example, consider the attribute temperature: A traditional decision tree might classify it as "Hot" if Temp > 30°C and "Cold" if Temp ≤ 30°C.A fuzzy decision tree defines overlapping categories like:

- Cold (0 to 20°C, max at 10°C)
- Warm (15 to 35°C, max at 25°C)
- Hot (30 to 50°C, max at 40°C)

A temperature of 28°C might belong to both "Warm (0.7)" and "Hot (0.3)", rather than a strict classification.

## 2. Constructing the Decision Tree

The decision tree is built similarly to traditional trees but uses fuzzy entropy or fuzzy information gain to determine the best attribute for splitting. Each internal node represents an attribute, and the edges correspond to fuzzy membership values rather than hard categorical splits. The algorithm selects the attribute that best reduces fuzzy uncertainty at each step.

## 3. Fuzzy Inference (Making Predictions)

Instead of assigning data points to a single class, FDTs use fuzzy inference rules to determine the probability of belonging to multiple classes. Each leaf node outputs a fuzzy class membership, which is then converted into a final decision using defuzzification techniques (such as weighted averaging or maximum membership).

Example of a Fuzzy Decision Tree Problem: Predicting Student Performance Based on Study Hours and Attendance

**Step 1:** Define Fuzzy Sets: Study Hours: {Low (0–3), Medium (2–6), High (5–10)}, Attendance: {Poor (0–40%), Average (30–80%), Good (70–100%)}, Performance (Class Labels): {Fail, Average, Excellent}

**Step 2:** Build the Fuzzy Decision Tree

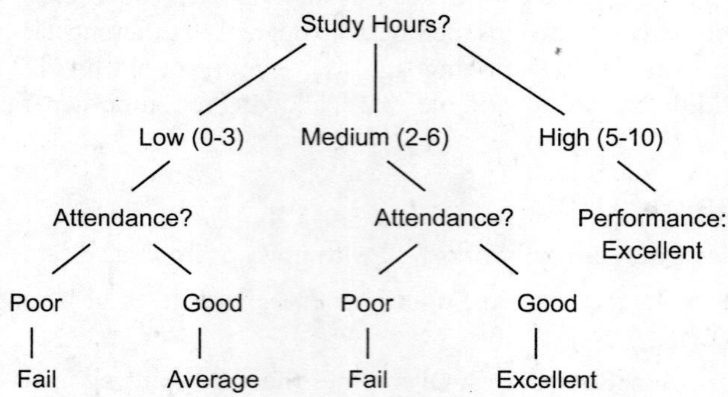


**Step 3:** Fuzzy Inference Example: A student with 4 study hours and 60% attendance might have the following membership values: Study Hours: Medium (0.8), High (0.2), Attendance: Poor (0.4), Good (0.6).Based on fuzzy rules, the student might have: Fail (0.2), Average (0.6), Excellent (0.2).The final decision is made using defuzzification (e.g., taking the highest membership value: "Average").

## Advantages of Fuzzy Decision Trees

- **Handles Uncertain and Imprecise Data:** Works well with noisy or ambiguous datasets.
- **Smooth Decision Boundaries:** Avoids abrupt transitions between categories.
- **Improved Interpretability:** Offers human-friendly, rule-based explanations.
- **Better Generalization:** Reduces overfitting by allowing partial membership in multiple classes.

## Challenges of Fuzzy Decision Trees

- **Computational Complexity:** Requires additional processing for fuzzy calculations.
- **Parameter Selection:** Choosing appropriate fuzzy membership functions is crucial.
- **Slower Training Time:** More complex calculations lead to increased training time compared to traditional trees.

## Applications of Fuzzy Decision Trees

- **Medical Diagnosis:** Handling vague symptoms like "mild fever" or "moderate pain."
- **Financial Risk Assessment:** Evaluating credit scores with uncertain data.
- **Customer Segmentation:** Categorizing customer preferences based on subjective feedback.
- **Weather Forecasting:** Predicting temperature variations with imprecise thresholds.
- **Industrial Process Control:** Managing uncertain conditions in manufacturing systems.

Fuzzy Decision Trees provide a powerful alternative to traditional decision trees by incorporating fuzzy logic, enabling them to handle uncertainty and overlapping class memberships. They are particularly useful in applications where rigid classification is not suitable, such as medical diagnostics, customer behavior analysis, and risk assessment. While they introduce additional computational complexity, their ability to model real-world ambiguity makes them a valuable tool in machine learning and artificial intelligence.

## UNIT SUMMARY

- This unit provides a comprehensive understanding of **clustering techniques and decision tree learning**, which are essential for machine learning and data analysis. Clustering is a form of **unsupervised learning** that groups data points with similar characteristics, while decision trees are a **supervised learning** approach used for classification and prediction. These techniques are widely applied in domains such as customer segmentation, fraud detection, medical diagnosis, and recommender systems.
- The unit begins with an **overview of clustering**, explaining its significance in data mining. Various **clustering methods** are explored, including **K-Means Clustering**, which is a widely used partition-based clustering algorithm, and **Fuzzy K-Means Clustering**, which assigns data points to multiple clusters with varying degrees of membership. The **Expectation-Maximization (EM) Algorithm** and **Gaussian Mixtures Clustering** are introduced as probabilistic clustering techniques that handle overlapping clusters effectively. Additionally, **Principal Component Analysis (PCA)** is covered as a dimensionality reduction technique that helps in optimizing high-dimensional datasets, while **Rough Sets-Based Methods** provide a rule-based approach to clustering, making them useful in dealing with uncertainty in data.
- The unit then shifts focus to **decision tree learning**, beginning with an **example of a classification decision tree**, which illustrates how trees split data into meaningful

categories. **Pruning** is discussed as a technique to remove unnecessary branches, improving model performance and reducing overfitting. Finally, **Fuzzy Decision Trees** are introduced, which integrate fuzzy logic into traditional decision trees, allowing them to handle uncertainty and imprecise data more effectively.

- By mastering clustering and decision tree learning, learners will be equipped to apply these techniques to real-world machine learning problems, improving data-driven decision-making and predictive analytics.

## EXERCISE

### 2-Mark Questions

1. Define clustering in machine learning.
2. What is the key difference between supervised and unsupervised learning?
3. List two advantages of using K-Means clustering.
4. What is the main difference between K-Means and Fuzzy K-Means clustering?
5. Define the Expectation-Maximization (EM) algorithm.
6. What is the role of Gaussian Mixture Models in clustering?
7. How does Principal Component Analysis (PCA) help in dimensionality reduction?
8. What are rough sets in machine learning?
9. What is the purpose of pruning in decision trees?
10. How do fuzzy decision trees differ from traditional decision trees?

### 16-Mark Questions

1. Explain the concept of clustering and discuss different types of clustering methods with examples.
2. Describe the working of the K-Means clustering algorithm and analyze its advantages and limitations.
3. Differentiate between K-Means and Fuzzy K-Means clustering with a real-world example.
4. Explain the Expectation-Maximization (EM) algorithm in detail and discuss its application in clustering.
5. Compare Gaussian Mixture Models (GMM) with K-Means clustering in terms of efficiency and accuracy.
6. Discuss the role of Principal Component Analysis (PCA) in feature selection and dimensionality reduction with an example.
7. Explain how rough sets-based methods are used for data classification and their significance in machine learning.
8. Construct a classification decision tree for a given dataset and explain its decision-making process.
9. Evaluate the importance of pruning in decision trees. Discuss different pruning techniques with examples.
10. Analyze the advantages of fuzzy decision trees over traditional decision trees and explain how they improve classification accuracy.

Unit 5

# Business Intelligence and Data Mining

## Rationale

In today's data-driven world, **Business Intelligence (BI) and Data Mining** are essential for organizations to gain actionable insights and enhance decision-making. This unit provides a comprehensive understanding of analytical techniques, data processing methods, and the latest trends in business intelligence and big data technologies.

The unit begins with **An Introduction to Analytics**, explaining its role in transforming raw data into valuable insights. It then covers the **CRISP-DM Model (Cross Industry Standard Process for Data Mining)**, which serves as a structured framework for implementing data mining projects efficiently. Understanding **Data Warehousing and Online Analytical Processing** (OLAP) is crucial, as these technologies enable organizations to store, retrieve, and analyze vast amounts of structured data for better business decisions.

Further, the unit explores **Mining Frequent Patterns and Association Rules**, which help in identifying relationships and patterns in large datasets, benefiting industries such as retail, healthcare, and finance. The concept of **Intelligent Information Retrieval Systems** is also introduced, focusing on techniques for efficiently searching and extracting relevant information from vast data sources.

The final sections discuss **Applications and Trends** in business intelligence, covering real-world use cases such as fraud detection, customer segmentation, and predictive analytics. Additionally, the unit delves into **Technologies for Big Data**, explaining advanced tools and platforms used to handle large-scale data processing. By the end of this unit, learners will have a strong foundation in business intelligence and data mining, enabling them to apply these concepts to real-world business challenges effectively.

## 5.1 INTRODUCTION TO ANALYTICS

In today's data-driven world, analytics plays a crucial role in decision-making across industries. Whether it's businesses tracking customer behaviour, healthcare professionals improving patient care, or sports teams analyzing performance, analytics helps make sense of complex data to drive smarter decisions.

### What is Analytics?

At its core, analytics is the process of examining data to uncover patterns, trends, and insights. It involves collecting, organizing, and analyzing information to support better decision-making. Think of it as a way to turn raw numbers into meaningful stories that help individuals and organizations take action.

### 5.1.2 Types of Analytics

Analytics can be broadly categorized into four types:

1. **Descriptive Analytics:** This answers the question, "What happened?" It involves summarizing past data to understand trends and performance. For example, a retailer analyzing last year's sales figures to identify best-selling products.
2. **Diagnostic Analytics:** This answers, "Why did it happen?" By drilling into past data, organizations can identify reasons behind successes or failures, such as why a marketing campaign performed better in one region than another.
3. **Predictive Analytics:** This focuses on "What might happen next?" Using historical data and statistical models, predictive analytics helps forecast future trends, like predicting customer demand for a product.
4. **Prescriptive Analytics:** This provides recommendations for "What should be done?" By using AI and machine learning, prescriptive analytics suggests actions to optimize outcomes, such as recommending the best price for a product to maximize profits.

### 5.1.3 Why is Analytics Important?

With the explosion of digital data, organizations that leverage analytics gain a competitive edge. It helps businesses improve efficiency, personalize customer experiences, reduce risks, and make well-informed strategic decisions. In everyday life, analytics also plays a role—whether in fitness apps tracking steps, financial tools managing budgets, or even streaming services recommending shows based on viewing habits.

## 5.2 THE CRISP-DM MODEL

CRISP-DM (Cross Industry Standard Process for Data Mining) is a widely used framework for executing data science and data mining projects. Developed in 1999, it provides a structured, step-by-step approach to handling data-related tasks and ensures consistency across projects.

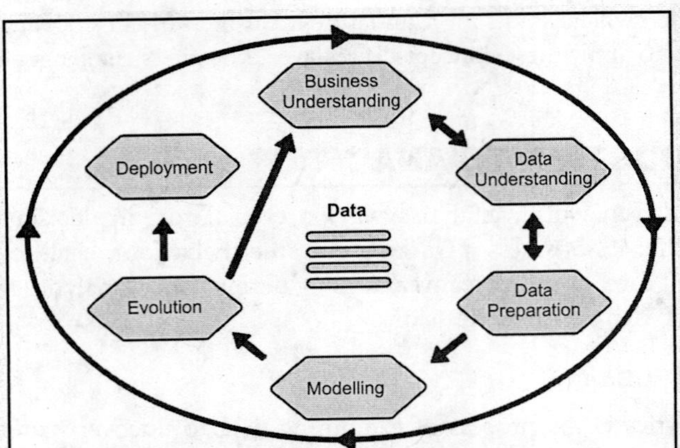


*Fig 5.1 Crisp Model*

### 5.2.1 Business Understanding Phase

The Business Understanding phase is all about clarifying the project's objectives and requirements. While many teams rush through this step, laying a solid foundation is as crucial as building the base of a house—it ensures stability and long-term success. With the exception of the third task, the remaining steps are fundamental project management activities applicable to most projects.

- **Define Business Objectives:** Identify what the client or organization aims to achieve, including key success criteria from a business perspective.
- **Evaluate the Situation:** Assess available resources, project requirements, potential risks, contingencies, and conduct a cost-benefit analysis.
- **Establish Project Goals:** Beyond defining business objectives, outline measurable success criteria from a technical and data mining standpoint.
- **Develop a Project Plan:** Choose appropriate tools and technologies while creating a detailed roadmap for each phase of the project.

### 5.2.2 Data Understanding Phase

Building on the foundation established in the Business Understanding phase, the Data Understanding phase focuses on identifying, gathering, and analyzing relevant datasets to support the project. This stage consists of four key tasks:

- **Acquire Initial Data:** Gather the necessary datasets and, if needed, load them into the appropriate analysis tools.
- **Describe the Data:** Review and document basic characteristics such as format, number of records, and field attributes.
- **Explore the Data:** Conduct deeper analysis through queries, visualizations, and relationship mapping to uncover patterns and insights.
- **Assess Data Quality:** Evaluate the cleanliness and completeness of the data, noting any inconsistencies or quality issues.

### 5.2.3 Data Preparation Phase

Often referred to as "data munging," this phase focuses on refining and structuring the data for modelling. It's typically the most time-consuming stage, with a general estimate that 50% to 80% of the total project effort goes into data preparation. This phase consists of five key tasks:

- **Select Data:** Identify which datasets will be used and document the rationale behind their inclusion or exclusion.
- **Clean Data:** This is often the most labour-intensive step. Ensuring data quality is crucial, as poor data leads to poor results. This process includes correcting errors, imputing missing values, and removing inconsistencies.
- **Construct Data:** Create new attributes or features that add value. For example, calculate Body Mass Index (BMI) from height and weight fields.
- **Integrate Data:** Merge multiple datasets to create a more comprehensive and usable dataset.
- **Format Data:** Adjust the data format as needed, such as converting string-based numerical values into numeric data types for analysis.

### 5.2.4 Modelling Phase

Modelling is often seen as one of the most exciting aspects of data science. In this phase, the team develops and evaluates different models, typically experimenting with multiple modelling techniques. While the CRISP-DM framework suggests iterating until the best possible model is found, in practice, teams often stop when they achieve a model that is "good enough" for the project's needs.

This phase consists of four key tasks:

- **Select Modelling Techniques:** Choose appropriate algorithms to apply, such as regression, decision trees, or neural networks.
- **Design Testing Strategy:** Depending on the modelling approach, split the dataset into training, testing, and validation subsets.
- **Build the Model:** Implement the chosen algorithm, often requiring just a few lines of code (e.g., reg = LinearRegression().fit(X, y)).
- **Evaluate the Model:** Compare multiple models and assess their performance based on domain knowledge, predefined success criteria, and test design.

### 5.2.5 Evaluation Phase

While the **Assess Model** step in the Modelling phase focuses on technical performance, the Evaluation phase takes a broader perspective—determining which model best aligns with business objectives and what actions to take next.

This phase consists of three key tasks:

- **Assess Results:** Do the models meet the business success criteria? Identify which model(s) should be approved for implementation.
- **Review the Process:** Reflect on the entire workflow. Were all steps executed correctly? Were any critical aspects overlooked? Summarize key findings and make necessary adjustments.
- **Decide Next Steps:** Based on the evaluation, determine whether to move forward with deployment, refine the models further, or explore new project directions.

### 5.2.6 Deployment Phase

A model is only valuable if its results can be effectively accessed and utilized. Deployment should be considered in terms of how the project's insights will be applied in practice. Depending on the scope, this could range from sharing a simple report to integrating a real-time predictive model into a production system.

This final phase consists of four key tasks:

- **Develop a Deployment Plan:** Outline and document the strategy for implementing the model.
- **Establish Monitoring & Maintenance:** Create a plan to track model performance and ensure long-term reliability during its operational phase.
- **Generate Final Report:** Summarize key findings, methodologies, and outcomes, often including a final presentation of results.
- **Conduct Project Review:** Reflect on the overall process, identifying successes, areas for improvement, and lessons for future projects.

## 5.3 DATA WAREHOUSING AND ONLINE ANALYTICAL PROCESSING

### 5.3.1 What is a Data Warehouse?

A **data warehouse** is a separate repository for storing and managing data, distinct from operational databases. According to William H. Inmon, a data warehouse is:

- **Subject-oriented:** Focuses on key business subjects like customers, products, or sales.
- **Integrated:** Combines data from multiple sources, ensuring consistency.
- **Time-variant:** Maintains historical data for long-term analysis.
- **Non-volatile:** Once data is added, it remains unchanged, supporting analytical processing.

Organizations use data warehouses for tasks such as customer behavior analysis, product performance assessment, and operational efficiency improvements.

### 5.3.2 OLTP vs. OLAP Systems

- **OLTP (Online Transaction Processing)** handles day-to-day operations like banking and payroll, focusing on fast transactions and real-time processing.
- **OLAP (Online Analytical Processing)** supports data analysis and decision-making, handling large amounts of historical data with complex queries.

| Feature | OLTP | OLAP |
|---|---|---|
| Users | Clerks, IT staff | Managers, Analysts |
| Data | Current, detailed | Historical, summarized |
| Design | ER model | Star/Snowflake schema |
| Access | Frequent, short transactions | Complex queries, read-heavy |

### 5.3.3 Why a Separate Data Warehouse?

Using a separate data warehouse improves performance by offloading complex queries from operational databases. OLAP queries require historical data and extensive aggregations, which can slow down operational systems.

### 5.3.4 Data Warehouse Architecture

- **Bottom Tier (Database Server):** Stores extracted, cleaned, and transformed data from various sources.
- **Middle Tier (OLAP Server):** Uses relational (ROLAP) or multidimensional (MOLAP) techniques for analysis.
- **Top Tier (Client Tools):** Includes reporting, data mining, and visualization tools for users.

### 5.3.5 Types of Data Warehouses

- **Enterprise Data Warehouse (EDW):** A central repository for the entire organization.

- **Data Mart:** A smaller, department-specific subset of a data warehouse.
  - *Independent Data Mart:* Built from external sources.
  - *Dependent Data Mart:* Extracted from an enterprise warehouse.
- **Virtual Warehouse:** A set of views over operational databases without separate physical storage.

### 5.3.6 Data Warehouse Development Approaches

- **Top-Down Approach:** Starts with an enterprise-wide warehouse and then builds data marts. Ensures integration but takes longer.
- **Bottom-Up Approach:** Starts with data marts and later integrates them. Faster and cost-effective but may lead to inconsistencies.
- **Recommended Method:** Develop in an **incremental and evolutionary manner**, combining both approaches.

### 5.3.7 ETL Process (Extraction, Transformation, Loading)

- **Extraction:** Collecting data from multiple sources.
- **Transformation:** Cleaning, converting, and standardizing data.
- **Loading:** Storing the processed data in the warehouse.
- **Refresh:** Updating the warehouse with new data periodically.

### 5.3.8 Data Warehouse Models

- **Star Schema:** A central fact table connected to dimension tables. Simple and widely used.
- **Snowflake Schema:** A variation where dimension tables are normalized. Reduces redundancy but requires more joins.
- **Fact Constellation (Galaxy Schema):** Multiple fact tables sharing dimension tables, used for complex applications.

### 5.3.9 Data Cube & OLAP Operations

A **data cube** allows multidimensional analysis. OLAP operations include:

- **Roll-up (Drill-up):** Aggregates data to a higher level (e.g., city → country).
- **Drill-down:** Moves from summary to detailed data (e.g., year → month).
- **Slice:** Filters data on a single dimension (e.g., sales in 2023).
- **Dice:** Filters data based on multiple dimensions (e.g., sales in Q1 for two cities).
- **Pivot:** Rotates data to view from different perspectives.

#### *Metadata in Data Warehousing*

Metadata describes the structure, content, and processing rules of a data warehouse, including:

- Data warehouse schema and attributes.
- Operational metadata (data sources, updates, error logs).
- Algorithms for summarization and aggregation.

## 5.3.10 Data Similarity & Dissimilarity Measures

To analyse relationships between data objects, similarity and dissimilarity measures are used:

- **Euclidean Distance:** Measures straight-line distance between two points.
- **Manhattan Distance:** Calculates distance in a grid-like pattern.
- **Cosine Similarity:** Used for text-based data, measuring the angle between two vectors.
- **Jaccard Coefficient:** Measures similarity between sets of attributes.

### *Statistical Data Descriptions*

Basic statistical measures help understand data distribution:

- **Mean, Median, Mode:** Measures central tendency.
- **Variance & Standard Deviation:** Indicates data spread.
- **Quartiles & Interquartile Range (IQR):** Helps detect outliers.
- **Boxplots & Histograms:** Visualize data distribution.

## 5.3.11 OLAP Operations

OLAP (Online Analytical Processing) allows users to explore and analyze data from multiple perspectives. One of its strengths is the use of **concept hierarchies**, which structure data at different levels of detail. Here are some of the most common OLAP operations:

- **Roll-up (Drill-up):** This operation moves data to a higher level of summarization. For instance, instead of viewing sales figures at the **city** level, you can roll them up to the **state** or **country** level. Another way to roll up data is by removing dimensions—for example, aggregating total sales by location instead of breaking them down by both **location** and **time**.
- **Drill-down:** The opposite of roll-up, drill-down provides a more detailed view. If you're looking at **yearly** sales data, you can drill down to see figures by **quarter, month, or even day**. Another way to drill down is by adding more dimensions to a dataset, offering deeper insights.
- **Slice and Dice:** These operations help refine data analysis:
  - ♦ **Slice** filters data based on a single dimension. For example, if you're analyzing sales performance, you might slice the data to focus only on **Q1 sales**. Figure 5.2 gives the example for slice.
  - ♦ **Dice** filters data using multiple dimensions at once. For instance, you might analyze sales data for specific **cities (Toronto, Vancouver)**, within a **specific timeframe (Q1, Q2)**, and for **specific product categories (home entertainment, computers)**.
- **Pivot (Rotate):** Pivoting changes the way data is viewed by switching dimensions for better visualization. For example, instead of seeing sales data organized by **products across locations**, you can pivot the view to compare **locations across products**.

These OLAP operations make it easier for businesses to analyze complex data, uncover trends, and make informed decisions.

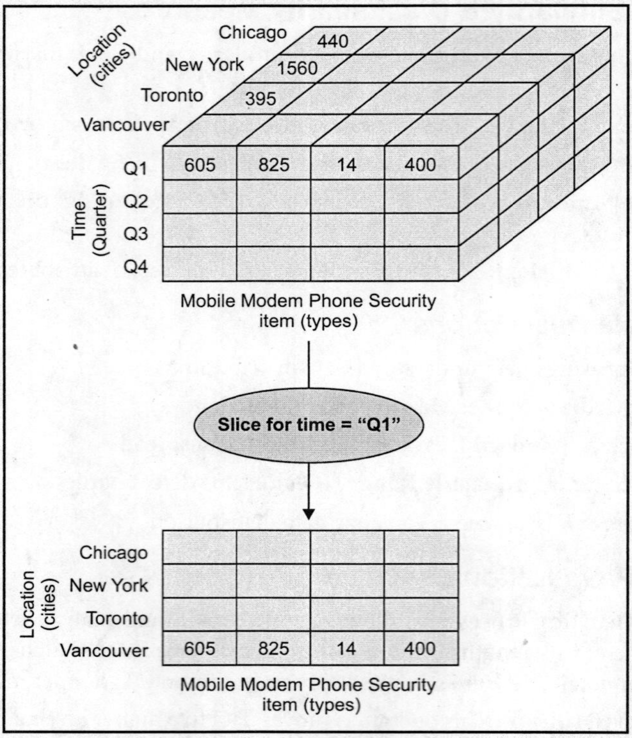


***Fig 5.2*** *Slice*

## 5.4 MINING FREQUENT PATTERNS AND ASSOCIATION RULES

Frequent patterns refer to recurring relationships in data, such as commonly purchased item combinations, sequential purchasing behaviors, or structural patterns in complex datasets. These patterns are fundamental in various data mining tasks like **association rule mining, clustering, and classification**.

### 5.4.1 Types of Frequent Patterns

- **Frequent Item sets:** Groups of items that often appear together in transactions (e.g., customers frequently buying **milk and bread** together).
- **Sequential Patterns:** Ordered sequences of events or purchases (e.g., buying a **PC → digital camera → memory card** in that order).
- **Structured Patterns:** Recurring substructures in data, such as **subgraphs, subtrees, or sublattices**, which may be combined with item sets or sequences.

### 5.4.2 Market Basket Analysis: A Real-World Application

Frequent pattern mining plays a crucial role in **market basket analysis,** where businesses analyse customer purchasing habits to find associations between products. Understanding these relationships helps companies optimize:

- **Product placement & catalogue design:** Arranging related items together to increase sales.
- **Cross-marketing strategies:** Recommending complementary products based on buying trends.
- **Customer behaviour analysis:** Identifying buying patterns to enhance targeted marketing.

With businesses collecting vast amounts of transaction data, uncovering frequent patterns allows for better decision-making, ultimately improving customer experience and boosting revenue.

### 5.4.3 Association Rules

In transactional databases, each transaction has a unique **Transaction ID (TID)** and contains a set of items. A **frequent itemset** is a group of items that appear together in transactions at least as often as a predefined minimum **support threshold** (*min sup*).

An **association rule** takes the form **A ⇒ B**, meaning that if a transaction contains **A**, it is likely to contain **B** as well.

- **Support (s)** measures how often **A and B appear together** in transactions:
  - support(A⇒B)=P(A∪B)
  - support(A ⇒ B) = P(A ∪ B)
  - support(A⇒B)=P(A∪B)
- **Confidence (c)** measures how often **B appears in transactions that contain A**:
  - confidence(A⇒B)=P(B|A)
  - confidence(A ⇒ B) = P(B | A)
  - confidence(A⇒B)=P(B|A)

Rules that meet both the **minimum support** and **minimum confidence** thresholds (*min conf*) are considered **strong rules** and are valuable for decision-making.

### 5.4.4 Types of Frequent Item Sets

- **Closed Frequent Item sets** – A frequent itemset **X** is considered *closed* if **no immediate superset of X has the same support as X.**
- **Maximal Frequent Item sets (Max-Item sets)** – An itemset is *maximal* if it is frequent, and **no larger superset of it is also frequent.**

### Process of Association Rule Mining

- **Find all frequent item sets** – Identify item combinations that appear frequently in transactions and meet the *min sup* threshold.
- **Generate strong association rules** – Use the frequent itemsets to create rules that satisfy both *min sup* and *min conf.*

## 5.5 INTELLIGENT INFORMATION RETRIEVAL SYSTEMS

An Intelligent Information Retrieval System (IIRS) is an advanced system that retrieves relevant information from large datasets using artificial intelligence (AI), machine learning (ML), and natural language processing (NLP) techniques.

These systems enhance search efficiency by understanding user queries, ranking results, and refining responses based on user preferences. They play a crucial role in search engines, recommendation systems, digital libraries, and enterprise knowledge management.

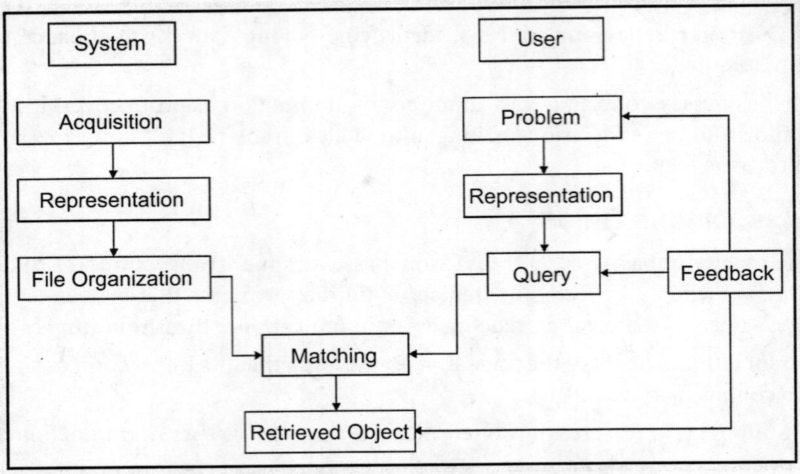


***Fig.5.3.** Intelligent Information Retrieval Systems*

*Figure 5.3 gives workflow of Intelligent Information Retrieval Systems*

## 1. Understanding Information Retrieval (IR)

Traditional Information Retrieval (IR) refers to the process of searching for relevant documents, images, or data from a collection. However, Intelligent IR systems go beyond keyword matching by understanding context, semantics, and user intent. They incorporate AI-driven approaches to rank and personalize results dynamically, improving search accuracy and efficiency. **Example:** Google's search engine uses intelligent retrieval algorithms to rank pages based on relevance, quality, and user engagement.

## 2. Components of an Intelligent IR System

An Intelligent Information Retrieval System typically consists of:

- **Data Indexing:** Organizing and structuring data for efficient retrieval.
- **Query Processing:** Understanding and refining user queries for better results.
- **Ranking and Scoring:** Assigning relevance scores to retrieved documents.
- **Feedback Mechanisms:** Learning from user behavior to improve future searches.

**Example:** Google Scholar indexes academic papers, allowing users to retrieve the most relevant research based on citations and author credibility.

## 3. Machine Learning in Intelligent IR

Machine learning algorithms improve IR systems by enabling automated learning and ranking. Supervised and unsupervised learning techniques are used to optimize search relevance. Deep learning models, like BERT (Bidirectional Encoder Representations from Transformers), understand complex language structures, making search results more contextually accurate.

**Example:** Amazon's product search engine uses ML models to personalize search results based on past purchases and browsing history.

## 4. Natural Language Processing (NLP) in IR

NLP enhances IR by allowing systems to interpret synonyms, sentence structures, and user intent rather than just matching keywords. Techniques like lemmatization, named entity recognition (NER), and word embeddings improve search accuracy.

**Example:** Google's RankBrain algorithm uses NLP to understand vague or ambiguous search queries and provide the most relevant results.

## 5. Semantic Search and Context Awareness

Semantic search focuses on understanding user intent and the contextual meaning of queries rather than simply matching words. This approach improves search accuracy by considering synonyms, related concepts, and knowledge graphs.

**Example:** IBM Watson Discovery helps enterprises extract insights by analyzing contextual relationships in business documents and reports.

## 6. Personalization and Adaptive Learning

Intelligent IR systems use user behavior tracking and adaptive learning to personalize search results. They analyze click patterns, browsing history, and feedback loops to refine recommendations over time.

**Example:** Netflix's recommendation engine personalizes movie suggestions by analyzing a user's viewing history and preferences.

## 7. Image and Video Retrieval Systems

Beyond text-based searches, visual information retrieval leverages AI-powered techniques such as convolutional neural networks (CNNs) and deep learning to retrieve images and videos based on patterns and objects.

**Example:** Google Lens allows users to search for objects in images using AI-powered visual recognition.

## 8. Challenges in Intelligent IR Systems

Despite advancements, Intelligent IR systems face challenges such as:

- **Data Overload:** Managing massive datasets efficiently.
- **Bias in Search Results:** Ensuring fair and unbiased ranking algorithms.
- **Real-time Processing:** Handling large-scale searches with minimal latency.
- **Multilingual Search:** Supporting diverse languages and dialects.
- **Example:** Bing and Google AI teams continuously refine their algorithms to reduce search bias and improve multilingual retrieval accuracy.

## 9. Applications of Intelligent IR Systems

Intelligent IR systems are widely used in:

- **Search Engines** (Google, Bing, Baidu) for fast and accurate web searches.

- **E-commerce Platforms** (Amazon, eBay) for personalized product recommendations.
- **Healthcare** (IBM Watson, PubMed) for medical research and diagnosis support.
- **Legal Research** (LexisNexis, Westlaw) for retrieving case laws and legal documents.
- **Digital Libraries** (Google Books, Project Gutenberg) for scholarly search and archiving.
- **Example:** PubMed helps doctors and researchers find relevant medical literature for diagnosis and treatment decisions.

## 10. Future of Intelligent Information Retrieval

The future of IR is driven by advancements in AI, deep learning, and quantum computing. Future IR systems will integrate:

- **Voice and Conversational Search:** AI-powered assistants like Siri and Alexa will improve spoken query understanding.
- **Augmented Reality (AR) Search:** Users can retrieve information using AR interfaces.
- **Federated Search Models:** Decentralized and privacy-focused search mechanisms.
- **AI-Powered Summarization:** Condensing search results into concise, meaningful summaries.
- **Example:** AI-powered summarization tools like Perplexity AI provide direct answers instead of long lists of search results.

Intelligent Information Retrieval Systems have revolutionized how users interact with vast data repositories. By integrating AI, ML, NLP, and semantic search techniques, these systems offer faster, more relevant, and personalized search experiences. As technology advances, the next generation of IR systems will provide even more intuitive and efficient ways to access and utilize information across multiple domains.

### 5.5.1 What Are Intelligent Information Retrieval Systems?

Intelligent Information Retrieval (IIR) systems use advanced algorithms, machine learning, and natural language processing (NLP) to efficiently find relevant information from vast datasets.

Unlike traditional search engines, these systems understand context, user intent, and relationships between data, improving the accuracy and relevance of search results.

### 5.5.2 Key Features of IIR Systems

- **Natural Language Processing (NLP):** Understands queries in a human-like manner rather than relying on exact keyword matches.
- **Machine Learning & AI:** Learns from user interactions to refine search results over time.
- **Semantic Search:** Goes beyond keyword matching to understand meaning and relationships between words.
- **Personalization:** Adapts search results based on user preferences, behavior, and search history.

- **Multimedia Retrieval:** Searches across text, images, audio, and video content.
- **Query Expansion & Refinement:** Suggests related terms and alternative queries to improve search accuracy.

### 5.5.3 How IIR Systems Work

- **Indexing & Preprocessing:** Data is collected, cleaned, and organized into structured formats for efficient retrieval.
- **Query Understanding:** The system analyzes user queries, identifying keywords, intent, and semantic meaning.
- **Ranking & Retrieval:** Relevant results are ranked based on **relevance scoring, machine learning models, and user feedback**.
- **Feedback & Learning:** The system refines results over time based on user interactions and preferences.

### 5.5.4 Applications of IIR Systems

- **Web Search Engines (Google, Bing):** Provides context-aware and personalized search results.
- **E-Commerce (Amazon, eBay):** Recommends products based on user behavior and search history.
- **Healthcare (Medical Information Retrieval):** Helps doctors find relevant research papers, case studies, and treatment guidelines.
- **Legal & Academic Research:** Assists in retrieving legal precedents, scientific papers, and patents.

## 5.6 APPLICATIONS AND TRENDS

Machine learning is an emerging technology that enables knowledge extraction from data. The first generation of machine learning algorithms including decision tree learning, fuzzy rule systems, neural networks, Bayesian classification, and logistic regression has already demonstrated significant value in various real-world data mining applications.

### 5.6.1 Mining Cyber-Physical System Data

Cyber-physical systems generate vast amounts of data from interconnected physical and digital components. For example, a **patient care system** links patient monitoring devices with medical records and emergency response systems. Similarly, **transportation networks** integrate real-time traffic monitoring using sensors and cameras, connecting to control systems for efficient traffic management.

### 5.6.2 Mining Multimedia Data

Multimedia data mining involves uncovering meaningful patterns from diverse media formats, including **images, videos, audio, graphics, and text**. This field combines **image processing, computer vision, data mining, and pattern recognition** to analyse and extract insights from multimedia databases.

### 5.6.3 Mining Web Data

The **World Wide Web** is an immense, ever-evolving repository of information, spanning news, advertisements, finance, education, government, and e-commerce. Web data mining extracts valuable insights from **hypertext structures, multimedia content, hyperlinks, and user access logs**, helping businesses and researchers make data-driven decisions.

## APPLICATIONS AND TRENDS IN APPLIED MACHINE LEARNING

Machine learning (ML) has evolved into a core technology that powers numerous real-world applications across various industries. With the advancement of deep learning, cloud computing, and AI automation, ML is continuously shaping the future of technology. Below, we explore **key applications** of applied machine learning, followed by emerging **trends** driving its evolution.

### Applications of Applied Machine Learning

#### *1. Healthcare and Medical Diagnosis*

Machine learning is transforming healthcare by improving disease detection, patient monitoring, and personalized treatment plans. Algorithms trained on medical datasets help in early diagnosis and predicting disease progression.

**Example: Google DeepMind's AI** can diagnose eye diseases from retinal scans with high accuracy, assisting doctors in early intervention.

#### *2. Fraud Detection and Cybersecurity*

Financial institutions and cybersecurity firms use machine learning to detect fraudulent transactions and cyber threats. ML models analyze transaction patterns to identify anomalies and alert authorities in real time.

**Example: PayPal and Mastercard** use ML to detect fraud by analyzing customer spending behavior and flagging suspicious transactions.

#### *3. Natural Language Processing (NLP) and Chatbots*

ML-driven **NLP models** enable machines to understand and generate human language, leading to intelligent chatbots and voice assistants. Companies use **chatbots** for customer service automation.

**Example: ChatGPT, Google Bard, and Amazon Alexa** use NLP to process and respond to user queries naturally.

#### *4. Self-Driving Cars and Autonomous Systems*

Machine learning powers autonomous vehicles by helping them perceive their environment, recognize objects, and make real-time driving decisions. **Deep learning models** process sensor data to navigate safely.

**Example: Tesla's Autopilot** uses ML algorithms for lane detection, traffic sign recognition, and collision avoidance.

#### *5. Recommender Systems in E-Commerce and Streaming Services*

ML-driven recommendation engines personalize content and product suggestions based on user preferences. These systems analyze user behavior, past purchases, and viewing history to improve engagement.

**Example: Netflix, Amazon, and YouTube** recommend movies, products, and videos using collaborative filtering and deep learning.

### 6. Financial Market Predictions and Algorithmic Trading

Machine learning is extensively used in finance for stock market prediction, risk assessment, and high-frequency trading. ML models analyze market trends, historical data, and real-time news to make investment decisions.

**Example: Hedge funds and investment firms** use ML-powered trading algorithms to automate buy/sell strategies.

### 7. Speech Recognition and Voice Assistants

Voice-enabled applications use ML to convert spoken language into text and execute commands. These systems continuously improve through deep learning models trained on vast speech datasets.

**Example: Siri, Google Assistant, and Cortana** use ML to improve speech recognition and natural conversation.

### 8. Predictive Maintenance in Manufacturing

Industries use machine learning to monitor equipment and predict failures before they occur. **IoT sensors** collect machine performance data, and ML models detect patterns indicating potential breakdowns.

**Example: General Electric** (GE) uses predictive maintenance to reduce downtime in industrial machines.

### 9. Agriculture and Precision Farming

ML in agriculture helps optimize crop production, monitor soil conditions, and detect diseases in plants. **Drone-based ML models** provide real-time data on crop health and irrigation needs.

**Example: John Deere** uses AI-powered tractors and drones to analyze farm conditions and improve yields.

### 10. Retail and Inventory Management

Retailers leverage ML to optimize inventory, predict demand, and enhance supply chain efficiency. AI models analyze customer purchasing patterns to manage stock levels effectively.

**Example: Walmart and Target** use machine learning to forecast demand and automate restocking.

## Emerging Trends in Applied Machine Learning

### 1. Automated Machine Learning (AutoML)

AutoML simplifies the ML model development process by automating feature engineering, model selection, and hyperparameter tuning. This trend is making machine learning accessible to non-experts.

**Example: Google AutoML** allows businesses to train custom ML models with minimal coding.

### 2. Explainable AI (XAI) and Ethical AI

As AI adoption grows, there is increasing demand for transparency in machine learning models. **Explainable AI (XAI)** helps interpret how ML models make decisions, ensuring fairness and reducing bias.

**Example: IBM Watson AI** provides explanations for its predictions, making AI decisions more understandable.

### 3. Edge AI and On-Device Learning

Edge AI refers to ML models running on **local devices** (e.g., smartphones, IoT devices) instead of cloud servers. This reduces latency, enhances privacy, and allows real-time processing.

**Example: Apple's Face ID and Google Lens** use on-device ML to process images without internet connectivity.

### 4. Federated Learning for Privacy-Preserving AI

Federated learning enables multiple devices to train ML models collaboratively without sharing raw data. This trend enhances **data privacy and security** in sensitive applications like healthcare and finance.

**Example: Google's Gboard keyboard** uses federated learning to improve text predictions without sending user data to the cloud.

### 5. TinyML: Machine Learning on Low-Power Devices

TinyML focuses on running ML models on **low-power microcontrollers** in embedded systems. This trend is driving innovation in **IoT devices, wearable tech, and smart sensors.**

**Example: Smart home devices like Nest thermostats** use TinyML for energy-efficient automation.

### 6. Generative AI and Transformer Models

Advancements in deep learning have led to powerful generative models that can **create text, images, music, and videos. Transformer architectures (GPT, BERT, DALL·E)** are driving AI creativity.

**Example: ChatGPT, Midjourney, and Stable Diffusion** generate human-like text and images.

### 7. Multimodal AI: Combining Different Data Types

Multimodal AI models integrate **text, images, audio, and video** into a unified learning system. These models improve AI applications in **healthcare, robotics, and virtual assistants**.

**Example: Google's Gemini AI** can process and generate insights across multiple data formats.

### 8. Self-Supervised and Few-Shot Learning

Traditional ML requires large labeled datasets, but self-supervised and **few-shot learning** allow models to learn with minimal supervision. This trend reduces the dependence on large training datasets.

**Example: OpenAI's CLIP** understands images and text with minimal labeled examples.

### *9. AI-Augmented Software Development*

Machine learning is automating software development by assisting in **code generation, debugging, and testing**. AI-powered **coding assistants** are boosting developer productivity.

**Example: GitHub Copilot and OpenAI Codex** suggest and generate code snippets based on natural language prompts.

### *10. Quantum Machine Learning (QML)*

Quantum computing is emerging as a game-changer for machine learning, enabling **faster computations and solving complex optimization problems** that classical computers struggle with.

**Example: Google's Quantum AI** is exploring quantum-enhanced ML algorithms for next-generation AI models.

Applied machine learning is revolutionizing industries by powering **automation, personalization, and intelligent decision-making**. From **healthcare and finance** to **self-driving cars and generative AI**, ML is expanding its influence across domains. Emerging trends like **AutoML, Explainable AI, Edge AI, and Quantum Machine Learning** will further **shape the future of AI-driven applications**, making technology more efficient, accessible, and ethical.

## 5.7 TECHNOLOGIES FOR BIG DATA

Big data technologies help businesses make smarter decisions by providing accurate insights, which improve efficiency, cut costs, and reduce risks. To handle massive amounts of structured and unstructured data in real-time, companies need a strong infrastructure that ensures data privacy and security.

### 5.7.1 Types of Big Data Technologies

Big data systems can be categorized into two main types:

#### *1. Operational Big Data*

These systems, such as MongoDB and NoSQL databases, are designed to handle real-time data processing. They focus on storing and managing large-scale data efficiently, making operations faster and more cost-effective. Many NoSQL databases allow businesses to analyze patterns and trends without requiring complex coding or specialized data science expertise.

#### *2. Analytical Big Data*

This category includes technologies like Massively Parallel Processing (MPP) databases and MapReduce, which specialize in deep analysis of historical data. These systems process large datasets by distributing tasks across multiple servers, making them highly scalable. Often, businesses use both operational and analytical systems together for a complete data-driven approach.

### Comparing Operational and Analytical Big Data Systems

| Feature | Operational Systems | Analytical Systems |
|---|---|---|
| Speed | Fast (Milliseconds) | Slower (Minutes to Hours) |
| Users | Customers & Apps | Data Scientists & Analysts |
| Function | Day-to-Day Operations | Deep Data Analysis |
| Data Type | Real-Time Transactions | Historical Data |
| Technology | NoSQL Databases | MapReduce, MPP Databases |

## Key Features of Big Data

Big data is commonly described using three major characteristics:

- **Volume:** The vast amount of data being generated every second.
- **Variety:** Different data formats like text, images, videos, and more.
- **Velocity:** The rapid speed at which data is produced and needs to be processed.

Big Data technologies refer to the tools, frameworks, and systems used to collect, store, process, and analyze vast amounts of data efficiently. As organizations generate increasing amounts of structured and unstructured data, specialized technologies have emerged to handle the **volume, velocity, and variety** of Big Data. Below, we explore some of the most significant Big Data technologies with examples.

### Hadoop: Distributed Data Processing

Apache Hadoop is one of the most widely used Big Data frameworks. It allows organizations to store and process large datasets across clusters of computers. Hadoop's HDFS (Hadoop Distributed File System) efficiently distributes data, while its MapReduce framework processes it in parallel.

**Example:** Companies like Facebook and Twitter use Hadoop to manage massive user-generated data such as posts, likes, and comments.

### Apache Spark: Real-time Data Processing

Apache Spark is a powerful alternative to Hadoop's MapReduce. It provides in-memory computing, making it much faster for processing large datasets. Spark supports multiple languages like Python, Scala, and Java and integrates with Hadoop, SQL, and machine learning libraries.

**Example:** Netflix uses Apache Spark for real-time customer recommendations based on user behavior.

### NoSQL Databases: Handling Unstructured Data

Unlike traditional relational databases, NoSQL databases are designed for flexible, high-speed data storage. These databases are essential for handling semi-structured and unstructured data, such as JSON, XML, and multimedia content. Popular NoSQL databases include:

- MongoDB (Document-based)

- Cassandra (Column-oriented)
- Redis (Key-value store)

**Example:** Instagram uses Cassandra to store billions of user interactions such as likes, comments, and follows.

### Data Lakes: Storing Raw Data

A Data Lake is a storage system that holds raw, unstructured, and structured data in its native format. Unlike traditional databases, Data Lakes provide flexible data storage without requiring pre-defined schemas.

**Example:** Amazon Web Services (AWS) S3 serves as a popular cloud-based Data Lake solution for organizations handling massive datasets.

### Data Warehouses: Structured Data Storage

A Data Warehouse is a centralized repository optimized for structured data storage and retrieval. It supports business intelligence and analytics by enabling fast querying and reporting. Examples include:

- Amazon Redshift
- Google BigQuery
- Snowflake

**Example:** Walmart uses Data Warehouses to analyze purchasing trends and optimize supply chain management.

### Apache Kafka: Real-time Data Streaming

Apache Kafka is a distributed event-streaming platform that processes real-time data flows. It allows businesses to ingest, store, and analyze high-velocity data from multiple sources.

**Example:** LinkedIn uses Kafka to track user activities such as page views, job applications, and messages.

### Apache Flink: Stream Processing Engine

Apache Flink is designed for real-time stream processing of Big Data. It can process continuous data streams with low latency, making it ideal for fraud detection, IoT applications, and stock market analysis.

**Example: Uber** uses Flink to process real-time location data for calculating surge pricing.

### TensorFlow and PyTorch: Big Data in AI and ML

Big Data plays a crucial role in artificial intelligence (AI) and machine learning (ML). TensorFlow and PyTorch are two leading deep learning frameworks used for training complex models on massive datasets.

**Example: Google Translate** uses TensorFlow to process and translate text in multiple languages using deep learning models.

### Apache Hive: SQL-Based Big Data Processing

Apache Hive provides a SQL-like interface for querying large datasets stored in Hadoop. It allows analysts to perform data summarization and analysis using familiar SQL commands.

**Example:** Airbnb uses Hive to analyze guest preferences and optimize booking recommendations.

### *Elasticsearch: Big Data Search Engine*

Elasticsearch is a powerful search and analytics engine that enables fast retrieval of structured and unstructured data. It is widely used for log analysis, full-text search, and anomaly detection.

**Example:** Wikipedia uses Elasticsearch to provide instant search results across millions of articles.

### *Apache Storm: Real-Time Analytics*

Apache Storm is an open-source framework for real-time analytics. It processes high-speed data streams, making it useful for tasks like fraud detection and sentiment analysis.

**Example:** Twitter uses Storm to analyze millions of tweets in real-time for trends and spam detection.

### *Google BigQuery: Cloud-Based Big Data Analytics*

Google BigQuery is a cloud-based data warehouse that allows organizations to analyze petabyte-scale datasets using SQL queries. It integrates with Google Cloud AI and machine learning services.

**Example:** Spotify uses BigQuery to analyze user listening habits and improve music recommendations.

### *Microsoft Azure HDInsight: Hadoop in the Cloud*

Azure HDInsight is a cloud-based Hadoop service that enables enterprises to process and analyze large-scale data using Spark, Hive, and Kafka. It allows organizations to scale their Big Data infrastructure on-demand.

**Example:** E-commerce platforms use HDInsight for real-time inventory management and customer behavior analysis.

### *Data Visualization with Tableau and Power BI*

Big Data technologies generate vast amounts of information, which must be visualized effectively. Tableau and Microsoft Power BI are two leading tools for creating interactive dashboards and reports.

**Example:** Financial institutions use Power BI to monitor stock market trends and analyze risk factors.

### *Future of Big Data Technologies*

The future of Big Data will involve increased adoption of AI-driven analytics, edge computing, and blockchain integration. Companies will continue leveraging these technologies to enhance decision-making, improve automation, and drive innovation across industries.

**Example:** Autonomous vehicles rely on real-time Big Data processing to make instant driving decisions using AI-powered sensors.

Big Data technologies have transformed industries by enabling efficient data storage, processing, and analysis. From Hadoop and Spark for large-scale computation to Kafka and Flink for real-time data streaming, organizations use these tools to extract meaningful insights. As AI, cloud computing, and real-time analytics evolve, the demand for Big Data technologies will continue to grow, shaping the future of data-driven decision-making.

## UNIT SUMMARY

- This unit provides a comprehensive overview of Business Intelligence (BI) and Data Mining, which are essential for extracting meaningful insights from large datasets to support strategic decision-making. It begins with An Introduction to Analytics, explaining how businesses leverage data-driven techniques to gain competitive advantages. Various types of analytics, including descriptive, predictive, and prescriptive, are discussed to highlight their importance in different industries.
- The unit then introduces the CRISP-DM Model (Cross-Industry Standard Process for Data Mining), a widely used framework that guides the structured implementation of data mining projects. Next, it covers Data Warehousing and Online Analytical Processing (OLAP), which are essential for organizing and analyzing large volumes of structured data, enabling efficient querying and reporting.
- A key focus of the unit is Mining Frequent Patterns and Association Rules, which help uncover hidden relationships within data. These techniques are particularly valuable in market basket analysis, fraud detection, and recommendation systems. The concept of Intelligent Information Retrieval Systems is also explored, highlighting methods for efficiently searching, filtering, and retrieving relevant data from vast information sources.
- The unit further discusses Applications and Trends in business intelligence, demonstrating how organizations use data mining for customer segmentation, financial forecasting, and healthcare analytics. Finally, Technologies for Big Data are introduced, covering modern tools and platforms such as Hadoop, Spark, and cloud-based analytics solutions that enable large-scale data processing. By the end of this unit, learners will have a solid understanding of BI and data mining techniques, equipping them with the skills to apply these methods in real-world business scenarios.

## EXERCISE

### 2-Mark Questions

1. What is the primary difference between descriptive and predictive analytics?
2. Define the term "analytics" in the context of data processing.
3. List two types of data analytics and provide a brief example of each.
4. What role does data quality play in the analytics process?
5. What does CRISP-DM stand for, and what is its purpose?
6. Mention the six phases of the CRISP-DM process.
7. Explain the importance of the 'Business Understanding' phase in the CRISP-DM model.

8. What is the purpose of the 'Data Preparation' phase in the CRISP-DM process?
9. What is a data warehouse, and why is it important for data analysis?
10. Define Online Analytical Processing (OLAP) and its key characteristics.
11. What is the difference between OLAP and OLTP?
12. Name any two components of a data warehouse architecture.
13. What are frequent patterns in data mining?
14. Explain the concept of an association rule in data mining.
15. What is the difference between support and confidence in the context of association rules?
16. Name one algorithm used for mining frequent patterns and briefly describe it.
17. What is an intelligent information retrieval system, and how does it differ from traditional information retrieval systems?
18. Name two techniques used in intelligent information retrieval.
19. What is natural language processing (NLP), and why is it important in intelligent information retrieval systems?
20. What role does machine learning play in intelligent information retrieval?
21. Provide two examples of applications of analytics in healthcare.
22. What is meant by "real-time analytics," and where is it commonly used?
23. Mention two current trends in the field of data analytics.
24. How does predictive analytics contribute to customer behavior analysis in retail?
25. What is big data, and how is it different from traditional data?
26. Name two technologies used for managing and analyzing big data.
27. What is Hadoop, and how does it support big data processing?
28. Explain the concept of "data lake" in the context of big data.

## 16 -Mark Questions

1. Explain the role of analytics in decision-making. Discuss how businesses use different types of analytics (descriptive, predictive, prescriptive) to make informed decisions.
2. Compare and contrast the four major types of analytics: descriptive, predictive, prescriptive, and diagnostic. Provide real-world examples for each and discuss how organizations can apply them.
3. Discuss the CRISP-DM model in detail. How does each of its phases contribute to the overall data mining process, and why is it considered one of the most widely used methodologies?
4. Critically evaluate the CRISP-DM methodology in comparison to other data mining models. What are its strengths and limitations in practical applications?
5. Explain the architecture of a data warehouse, detailing the functions of each layer. How do data warehouses support decision-making in businesses?
6. Discuss OLAP and its functionalities in depth. Compare different OLAP operations (e.g., slicing, dicing, drilling) and their role in analyzing multi-dimensional data.

7. Discuss the process of mining frequent patterns and association rules. Explain the significance of algorithms like Apriori and FP-growth in discovering useful patterns in large datasets.
8. Evaluate the effectiveness of association rule mining in different industries such as retail, healthcare, or finance. Provide examples of how businesses leverage association rules to enhance their strategies.
9. Discuss the principles behind intelligent information retrieval systems and how they differ from traditional keyword-based search systems. What are the key technologies used in intelligent information retrieval?
10. Explain how intelligent information retrieval systems use natural language processing and machine learning to improve search results. Illustrate with examples from industries like e-commerce or online search engines.
11. Analyze the current trends in data analytics and discuss how they are transforming industries such as healthcare, finance, and marketing. What are the challenges and opportunities associated with these trends?
12. Evaluate the future applications of big data analytics and artificial intelligence in different sectors. Discuss the potential impact of these technologies on business strategies and decision-making.
13. Explain the key technologies used in big data analytics, such as Hadoop and Spark. How do these technologies address the challenges of processing large volumes of unstructured data?
14. Discuss the role of cloud computing in enabling big data analytics. Evaluate the advantages

❖❖❖

*Intentionally left blank!*